TELL ME ABOUT
HISTORY

An Hachette UK Company
www.hachette.co.uk

First published in Great Britain in 2016 by Chancellor Press,
a division of Octopus Publishing Group Ltd
Carmelite House, 50 Victoria Embankment, London EC4Y 0DZ
www.octopusbooks.co.uk

Edited and designed by Anna Southgate and Leah Germann

ISBN 978-0-7537-3029-4

A CIP catalogue record for this book is available from the British Library

Printed and bound in China

10 9 8 7 6 5 4 3 2

Publisher: Lucy Pessell
Design Manager: Megan van Staden
Editor: Natalie Bradley
Production Controller: Sarah Kulasek-Boyd

UPDATED & REVISED

TELL ME ABOUT

HISTORY

ANSWERS TO HUNDREDS OF
FASCINATING QUESTIONS

CHANCELLOR
PRESS

CONTENTS

ANCIENT
CIVILIZATIONS

CONTENTS

WHO WERE THE FIRST HUMANS?

From fossils, scientists have discovered that the first human-like mammals lived on the eastern side of Africa at the beginning of the Pleistocene. We can trace our ancestry through fish, amphibians, mammal-like reptiles, primitive shrew-like mammals, lemur-like early primates, monkey-like forms and ape-like forms to a stage where distinctive human features begin to appear – upright posture, nimble hands and the ability to make and use tools. Our upright stance was probably due to several factors, including the fact that a brain at the top of a vertical spinal column would have a better chance to enlarge than one at the end of a horizontal one.

SOME OF OUR EARLIEST ANCESTORS MEASURED AROUND 1.2M (4FT) TALL WHEN STANDING UP. THAT'S ABOUT THE SAME HEIGHT AS A CHIMPANZEE!

• FACT FILE •

The most important of our immediate ancestors is Australopithecus. *Australopithecus afarensis* is one of the earliest known human species, and lived over three million years ago. The remains of some 300 of them have been found to date.

WHEN WAS THE STONE AGE?

Stone Age man (known as Neanderthal man) lived in Europe from about 100,000 to 35,000 years ago. During this time, people sheltered in caves and hunted animals using stone tools and wooden spears.

The early stone-crafting techniques of these people show surprising skill. They chipped or flaked off bits of stone to make shaped tools including hand axes and knives. Both the hand axe and scraper were usually made from flint, while spearheads were often shaped from wood or deer antlers.

The Stone Age hunters killed deer and other animals with spears, bows and stones, often ambushing them on the move. Although they were not as fast as the animals they hunted, they made up for it by using teamwork and accuracy with their weapons.

It was also around this time that people discovered how to make fire by using a simple wooden stick called a fire drill. The drill was turned quickly over a piece of dry wood until it produced enough heat to start the fire.

Historians call this period of prehistory the Stone Age, because stone was the most important material used by the first tool-makers.

WHERE WAS SUMER?

About 7,000 years ago, farmers began to move into an area of land between the Tigris and the Euphrates Rivers. This fertile land was called Mesopotamia, in what is now called Iraq. In the south of Mesopotamia was the land known as Sumer. It had little rain and long, hot summers. People had lived in Sumer since around 5000 BCE.

The Sumerians, as they became known, were a very intensive race. They fished the rivers, hunted wild pigs and birds for food, and picked fruit from date palms. The muddy soil was rich, but crops died without rain in the burning summer heat, so farmers dug canals to channel river water to their fields of barley, wheat, dates and vegetables. They turned over the earth with ploughs pulled by oxen. Skilled metalworkers in Sumer made fine trinkets from silver and gold. These items were inlaid with precious stones, such as lapis lazuli.

Sumerian robes

Sumerian body ornaments

Some of the wedge-shaped ('cuneiform') characters in the Sumerian writing system looked like objects, others were symbols.

FACT FILE

The Sumerians developed the first form of writing and recording numbers. They drew pictures on soft clay with a pointed reed. The pictures were drawn downwards in lines, from the right-hand side. Later, they started to write across the tablet from left to right.

WHICH WAS THE WORLD'S FIRST GREAT CIVILIZATION?

Various artefacts have been excavated in the Indus Valley, including vessels and toys made from copper, terracotta and bronze.

The Indus Valley civilization was one of the world's first great societies. It developed out of farming and herding communities that carried on trade with each other. The civilization began to flourish about 4,500 years ago and was based in the vast river plains of what are now Pakistan and northwestern India. There were two main cities – Harappa in the north of the Indus Valley and Mohenjo Daro in the south. They were both carefully planned cities and laid out on a grid system. They had wide roads and brick houses, most of which had at least two storeys. Most homes had a bathing area that was supplied with water from a nearby public well or from a well in the courtyard of the house. The people who lived there were farmers, tending to fields and watering crops with silt-laden waters washed down when the snows melted in the mountains to the north.

• FACT FILE •

The farmers of the Indus Valley used wooden carts pulled by pairs of oxen. We know this, because deep grooves made by heavily laden carts have been found in the excavated streets of Mohenjo Daro.

WHICH ANCIENT CIVILIZATION USED HIEROGLYPHICS?

Egyptian picture writing is known as hieroglyphics. This language is made up of about 750 signs, with pictures of people, animals and objects. Until hieroglyphics were deciphered in modern times, it was not known that most of the pictures represented sounds and syllables, not whole words. Scribes used a quick form of writing, which was called hieratic. The ancient Egyptians lived in the Nile area of north Africa in around 3000 BCE. They were good at maths, particularly geometry, which they used in architecture – for building their temples and pyramids – and surveying. They drew up an accurate 12-month calendar of 365 days, and used water clocks to measure time.

Papyrus showing the Pharaoh Tutankamen and gods Osiris, Hathor and Isis

FACT FILE

It wasn't until the discovery of the Rosetta Stone, which contained the same inscription in hieroglyphics and in Greek, that the meaning of these complicated pictures could be understood.

A detail from the tomb of Tutankhamen

WHO WERE THE MYCENEANS?

The Myceneans were warlike people who lived in Greece, possibly from around 1900 BCE. By 1600 BCE they were trading in the Aegean, and after the fall of Crete they became the major power in the region.

The Mycenean rulers lived in hilltop citadels overlooking cities protected by thick stone walls. The city of Mycenae was at the heart of their civilization. People entered Mycenae through the Lion Gate, a great stone gateway from which a path led straight to the royal palace. Graves of the ruling family, filled with treasure and personal possessions for the afterlife were discovered here in 1876.

Weakened by interstate warfare, the Mycenean cities were destroyed and lost. During an excavation of the graves at Mycenae in the late 1800s, the so-called 'mask of Agamemnon' was uncovered. It is unclear of the origin of this mask because so much of the cities and their history were destroyed, but it is believed to be the mask of an earlier king.

The mask of Agamemnon

The mask of Agamemnon is made of gold and is one of five masks to have been unearthed at Mycenae. A funeral mask would have been placed over the face of a person when buried.

• FACT FILE •

The Myceans had forms of writing that they used in business and government. They wrote on clay tablets and possibly also in ink on papyrus, like the Egyptians.

WHO WERE
THE ANCIENT GREEKS?

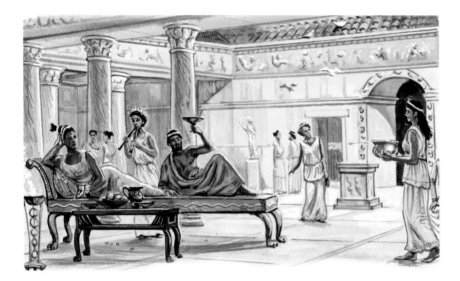

Ancient Greece is often considered the birthplace of modern civilization. Much of what we know about the ancient Greeks comes from pictures on vases, which show daily activities such as hunting, farming and fishing. Greek homes were built around a central courtyard, where the family slaves prepared food on an open fire. There was a small shrine to the household god. Many houses were built without windows, keeping out both the hot sun and thieves. People ate with their fingers while lying on wooden couches. Slaves brought in food, while a musician played on pipes or a lyre. Men and women wore a chiton – that is, a cloth square draped over the body and fastened by a pin at the shoulder.

? DID YOU KNOW THAT THE GREEKS INVENTED THE OLYMPIC GAMES? THE GAMES STARTED AS A RELIGIOUS FESTIVAL HELD IN HONOUR OF ZEUS, KING OF THE GODS. THE FESTIVAL TOOK PLACE AT OLYMPIA, BELOW MOUNT OLYMPUS, EVERY FOUR YEARS.

WHO WERE
THE OLMECS AND CHAVINS?

Two groups made up America's earliest civilizations – the Olmecs in Mexico and Central America, and the Chavins in Peru on the west coast of South America.

The Olmecs flourished between c. 1500 and 400 BCE. They made pottery, cleared the jungle to grow crops and constructed large stepped pyramids from earth. They held religious ceremonies and built temples for their gods on top of their pyramids.

The Chavins who lived in the foothills of the Andes became farmers by about 1000 BCE. They built the first towns in South America. They cut terraces into hillsides and became expert at irrigation in order to cultivate the dry land of the mountain slopes.

THE OLMECS ARE BEST KNOWN FOR MASSIVE CARVED STONE HEADS THAT REMAIN AT A NUMBER OF THEIR ARCHAEOLOGICAL SITES. THE LARGEST IS 3M (10FT) TALL AND WEIGHS AROUND 40 TONNES!

FACT FILE

In modern Peru, craftworkers carry on the traditions of their Chavin ancestors, producing woven textiles like this basket. Designs such as these have been produced in Peru for around 3,000 years.

WHERE WAS ETRURIA?

Etruria was an area of Italy, known today as Tuscany, Umbria and Latium. Etruria extended from the Arno River in the north to the Tiber River in the south, and from the Apennine Mountains in the east to the Tyrrhenian Sea in the west. It is believed that the Etruscans migrated to Etruria in about 800 BCE from the east, probably travelling by sea. In Etruria, the Etruscans made near-slaves of the people who lived there. The Etruscans then spread north across the Apennines into the Po Valley and south across the Tiber River into Latium and Campania. The civilization reached its height in the 7th and 6th centuries BCE, but in about 510 BCE the Etruscan kings were driven out of Rome, which then became a republic.

? DID YOU KNOW THAT THE ANCIENT ETRUSCANS WERE THE FIRST MEDITERRANEAN CIVILIZATION TO ADOPT A GRID PLAN FOR THEIR CITIES?

• FACT FILE •

Part of a carved stone relief depicting a Roman funeral procession. The pallbearers carried the dead person on a raised bier, followed by the mourners.

WHO WERE THE ASSYRIANS?

The country once known as Mesopotamia covered roughly the northern part of present-day Iraq.

Assyria was an ancient country on the upper Tigris River in Mesopotamia. The people who lived there were called Assyrians and they were ruled by a king called Ashurbanipal from 668 to 627 BCE. Ashurbanipal was the last great Assyrian ruler. He made the city of Nineveh his capital. Here he oversaw the building of a magnificent palace, a library and ornate gardens.

The Assyrian chief god was Assur, and the king was regarded as Assur's representative on Earth. The king was in charge of the army and the government, and he also controlled the temples and their priests. Residents of some of the older cities, such as Assur and Nineveh, enjoyed special privileges, including low taxes and freedom from military service. Landlords had to pay taxes and provide young men from their estates to serve in the army. Beyond Assyria itself, the empire was divided into provinces. Each province was administered by a governor who was responsible to the central government.

• FACT FILE •

Assyrian artists made wall relief sculptures showing winged spirits, hunting scenes, lions and bulls. For sport, the Assyrian king and his nobles would kill captive lions released into special enclosures.

WHO WERE THE FIRST SETTLERS OF JAPAN?

People from mainland Asia had settled on the islands of Japan by 7000 BCE. The original inhabitants may have been the Ainu, about 15,000 of whom still live in Japan. The early Japanese lived by hunting and fishing. Farming began around 1000 to 500 BCE, when the Japanese began to grow rice, a skill learned from the Chinese. They also began to make metal tools and pottery using a potter's wheel.

The site in Tokyo where pottery was first found gives this period of history its name – Yayoi. The Yayoi farmers dug ditches to irrigate their rice fields. They built thatched homes and storehouses on stilts for their rice crops. Farmers lived together in villages, and each village was led by a chief who was often a woman shaman, or magician. Traditionally, the women shamans of Japan were extremely powerful figures.

During Japan's Yayoi period, the dead were often buried inside stone tombs.

• FACT FILE •

Each year the Japanese town of Nikko holds a festival that dates back to the 8th century. Called the Yayoi Festival, it takes place in April and is a celebration of spring. People dress in traditional costume and join a parade through the city's streets.

WHY DID ANCIENT CHINA HAVE SUCH ADVANCED CIVILIZATION?

An ancient Chinese wheelbarrow with a wheel that was added much later

IT IS THANKS TO THE ANCIENT CHINESE THAT WE HAVE FIREWORKS! THEY INVENTED GUNPOWDER AS EARLY AS THE FIRST CENTURY. LATER, IN AROUND 1200, THEY FILLED BAMBOO TUBES WITH GUNPOWDER AND FIRED THEM AS ROCKETS AT THEIR ENEMIES.

Chinese cities were a wonder to foreign visitors. Chang'an had more than one million citizens, yet its cleanliness was startling. There were public baths, and hot water was sold in the streets for washing. Toilet facilities in houses were fairly basic, emptying into cesspits, but waste was collected in carts every evening and taken away. The Chinese habit of using toilet paper came as another surprise to visitors.

The Chinese were fascinated by machines. They invented the wheelbarrow for carrying loads, and even fitted barrows with sails to make pushing easier. They used waterwheels to mill rice and hammers to beat metal into shape. They knew about the magnetic compass, and their ships had stern rudders. Chinese soldiers had the best crossbows in the world, and smoke and fire weapons.

• FACT FILE •

A paper-maker at work, spreading wet pulp over a mesh frame. The invention of paper was announced by the director of the Chinese imperial workshops in 105 CE. The Chinese began to use paper money in about 800 CE.

WHO WERE THE ANCIENT ROMANS?

The ancient Romans were one of the world's great historic civilizations, founded in the 8th century BCE, and growing to be a vast empire. Among the things the Romans are best remembered for are their impressive villas and public baths and their gladiator sports.

A Roman villa was a large, comfortable country home, with hot-air central heating and a courtyard for fine weather. The family had servants to run the house and slaves to work on the land. Only the wealthiest Romans could afford their own baths, so many cities had public baths as well. These became luxurious meeting places. They looked like large square or rectangular swimming pools, and were surrounded by gardens, columned marble alcoves and libraries. The bath buildings had facilities for warm and cold baths, steam baths and massages.

The first gladiator games were held in a Roman cattle market in 264 BCE.

Gladiators were trained warriors who fought bloody battles to entertain the ancient Romans. Gladiators fought using many different types of weapons – a shield and sword, a net and a long three-pronged spear, for example. They usually fought until one of them was killed, but the life of the loser could be spared if the spectators waved handkerchiefs.

FACT FILE

Roman chariot races were fast and furious, with frequent violent crashes, and winning drivers becoming rich superstars. In more recent times, race tracks, indoor circuses and amusement places have been called hippodromes.

WHY DO WE KNOW SO LITTLE ABOUT CELTIC CULTURE?

The Celts came from Central Europe, although their previous origins are unclear. Around 500 BCE, perhaps to escape wars with their Germanic neighbours, they began to move westwards. Groups of people settled in what are now Spain, France, Britain and Ireland. Celts were warlike and their arrival usually led to fighting.

The Celts were artistic people. They loved stories and music, and they made beautiful jewellery and metalwork decorated with abstract designs and animal shapes.

They had no written language, passing on their legends of gods and heroes in stories around the fire. Most of what we know of the Celts today comes from the writings of their enemies, such as the Romans. The Celts themselves left a legacy of art and legend, and language: Welsh, Breton, Cornish, Irish and Scottish Gaelic are all Celtic languages.

• FACT FILE •

The Celts often constructed their settlements on hilltops, which could be easily defended. The settlements are identified by circular defensive ditches that still survive in former Celtic areas.

THE CELTS WERE HEAD-HUNTERS AND BELIEVED THAT THE GREATEST PRIZE IN BATTLE WAS THE SEVERED HEAD OF THEIR ENEMY!

An example of typical Celtic art.

WHO WERE THE FRANKS?

When the Roman Empire collapsed, the Franks emerged in 476 CE, as the dominant force in western Europe. The 'Franks' were made up of a group of tribes, living north and east of the Lower Rhine River in Western Germany. Clovis the First extended his territory by conquest, with the aid of the peasant farmers who owed military service to the noble landowners. This system of land holding and service may have formed the basis of European feudalism. By the year 540 CE the Franks ruled most of the old Roman province of Gaul (modern-day France). 'Franks' means 'free' as the Franks of Gaul were free of taxation. The ruling family, known as the Merovingian dynasty, is named after Clovis's grandfather Merovaeus. Clovis became a Christian and made Paris his capital city. The Holy Roman Emperor, Charlemagne, was king from 768 to 814. After his death the Frankish Empire began to break up.

DID YOU KNOW THAT THE NAME FOR FRANCE COMES FROM THE FRANKISH PEOPLE?

• FACT FILE •

The Frankish King Charlemagne introduced this writing, called 'Carolingian script', which was easier for people to read and write.

WHEN DID THE VIKINGS PROGRESS THROUGH EUROPE?

Ships moored beside a Viking coastal town

Viking men and women used decorative brooches to hold their outer garments (cloaks and tunics) in place.

The Vikings came from Scandinavia (Norway, Denmark and Sweden). Their homelands offered little spare farmland for a growing population, so many Vikings went abroad in search of new lands. The Vikings were farmers, but also fierce warriors, and their first impact on western Europe was a violent one. They began to sail across the North Sea in the late 700s CE, raiding the coasts of Britain and mainland Europe. They raided churches and towns, carrying off loot and slaves. Their raids caused panic, and rulers tried to buy off the invaders with gold. This, however, only encouraged the Vikings to come back for more.

WHEN WAS
THE START OF SAXON BRITAIN?

In the late 300s CE the Roman army was hard-pressed to fight off waves of barbarian invasions. Troops in distant outposts, such as the British Isles, were needed to defend the empire, and by 410 CE the last Roman soldiers had left England for mainland Europe.

Without the Roman army to protect them, the Roman Britons of England were unable to prevent these mercenaries, and any new bands of invaders, from taking over land they wanted. The newcomers were a mixture of people – Angles, Saxons, Jutes, Frisians – who became known as the 'English'. The invaders came to England to find land to farm. They were well-armed and tough, and drove away many Britons, who moved into western England.

Saxon farmers

The Saxons settled in several kingdoms, including Northumbria, East Anglia, Essex, Sussex, Wessex, Kent and Mercia.

FACT FILE

Treasures unearthed from a burial site at Sutton Hoo, Suffolk, included a gold belt, a sword and shield, an iron helmet, and several items of jewellery. Finally there was a sceptre and standard, which must have belonged to the dead King Redwald.

WHO WERE THE NORMANS?

The events of the Battle of Hastings were recorded in picture form in the Bayeux Tapestry, an embroidered fabric that measures almost 70m (230ft) in length.

The Normans were the followers of William the Conqueror, who defeated King Harold at the Battle of Hastings in 1066 to become King of England. William was French, and came from Normandy in northwestern France. The Normans introduced the feudal system, in which the king owned all the land, some of which he gifted to barons, in return for services to him.

The baronial estates were taken from the English earls. The barons paid taxes to the crown and supplied soldiers for the king's armies. The barons gifted smaller portions of their land to knights, for which they received military service. The knights let even smaller parcels of land to farmers who had to provide the knights with fresh food. Society was thus divided into easily controlled units. The Normans brought medieval French into the language and built many castles and churches.

• FACT FILE •

Knights were soldiers in the service of a Norman lord. They owed their loyalty to their lord and had to fight for him whenever asked. This meant that the knights were called upon in times of unrest.

WHO WERE THE AMERICAN INDIANS?

Mesa Verde is an archaelogical site in the United States and was once home to an ancient Native American community.

The American Indians were the native tribes living in America before the new settlers arrived from Europe from the end of the 15th century onwards. Large numbers of settlers made homes in the native American hunting and grazing lands, challenging their lifestyle and traditions. As the population of the United States grew rapidly, the Native Americans were forced to migrate to the south and west. Soon they had nowhere left to go and began to fight back. The US government reacted by forcing the Native Americans into reservations on land that was not wanted by the settlers. Many died fighting trying to save their land, or from starvation and disease. The huge herds of buffalo on which many depended were hunted by the settlers, depriving them of their main source of food, clothing and shelter.

• FACT FILE •

The American flag was originally designed with 13 stars and 13 stripes to represent the original colonies that signed the Declaration of Independence. With each new state, another star is added to the flag.

WHO ARE THE MAORI?

The Maori people were the first settlers in New Zealand. They arrived from Polynesia around 1,000 years ago. Today the Maori number over 300,000 and Maoritanga, the Maori language, is used by many people. Many ancient traditions are still maintained, such as *ta moko*, Maori tattooing. Many Maori men tattoo their faces and their bodies. The traditional *haka* dance can also be seen. It was originally performed at the onset of war to unite the people. Leg, arm, foot, hand and even tongue movements are all important in the *haka*.

A traditional Maori warrior carving in New Zealand

• FACT FILE •

There is more to a Maori man's tattoo than meets the eye. Tattoos on the face represent lineage – where a man comes from and important events in his life. Some Maori women have such tattoos, too, although this is relatively rare.

THE MAORI'S ARE PARTICULARLY KNOWN FOR THEIR WOODCARVING. THEY HAVE BUILT WOODEN WAR CANOES THAT ARE BIG ENOUGH TO CARRY 100 PEOPLE!

ANCIENT SITES AND STRUCTURES

CONTENTS

WHY WAS THE MEGALITHIC ERA SO-CALLED?

More than 5,000 years ago Europeans were building spectacular stone monuments. Many of these are still standing today, as mysterious relics of a long-gone society.

These enormous stones are called megaliths (literally 'big stones'). Some were set up on their own, others in groups or in circles. Some megaliths marked the burial place of an important ruler, while others seem to have had a religious meaning.

Tall single stones (menhirs), stone slab-tombs (dolmens) and the remains of large circles of stones and wooden posts (henges) are still standing today. Stonehenge is an example of remainders from the Megalithic era.

Megathithic tombs were also known as a dolmens or barrows. The one pictured on this page is situated between Penzance and Zennor in West Cornwall.

• FACT FILE •

Rock tombs, slab tombs (pictured) and stone circles and temples lie scattered across Europe. Many have been discovered on the island of Malta.

WHY WAS STONEHENGE BUILT?

Stonehenge

When we try to learn of the accomplishments of ancient man, we usually have to search or dig for evidence. But there is a case where all the evidence has been left standing in a huge structure, and we still cannot figure out what it is, what it was used for, and exactly who built it! This is Stonehenge. It is a complicated structure on the outside of which is a circular ditch, with an entrance gap.

Stonehenge was built in stages between 1800 and 1400 BCE. During the second stage of building, blue stones from the Preseli mountains in Wales were hauled onto the site in an astonishing feat of organization and transport. Local stones were added in the third stage and were up to 10m (32.8ft) long and weighed 50 tonnes (55 tons).

The Stonehenge builders had only stone or bronze tools to work with. They had no machines and yet they tackled huge digging works. They buried their chieftains, with treasures and food for the next world, beneath mounds of earth they called dolmens or barrows.

IN RECENT YEARS, STONEHENGE HAS ATTRACTED MORE THAN ONE MILLION VISITORS, ANNUALLY!

WHERE WOULD YOU HAVE SEEN A HOME MADE OF MAMMOTH BONES?

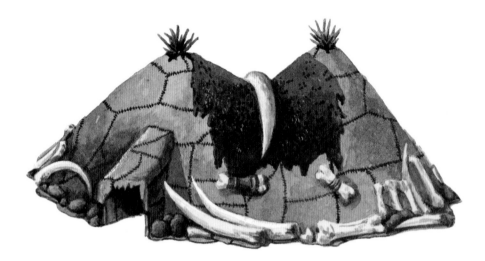

Mammoths are ancient relatives of the modern-day elephant. They were similar in size and had long curved tusks. Some of them also had a coating of shaggy hair. They have been extinct for centuries.

Around 18,000 years ago, the last in a series of Ice Ages gripped much of the northern hemisphere. Icecaps spread southwards across Europe and North America. The sea level fell, uncovering land bridges which animals and people crossed – from Asia to Alaska for example.

Ice Age hunters, clothed only in animal skins, adapted to living in these freezing conditions. They built shelters from the bones of mammoths. They made the framework from the bones and filled in the gaps with skins, turf and moss. Groups of men drove the animals into swamps, where they became trapped. Once there, they killed them using spears or rocks.

• FACT FILE •

Tools for scraping the skins of a hunted animal were made mostly from flint. This hard material could be chipped into useful tools of many different shapes and sizes. Other tools were made from bone, antlers and tusks.

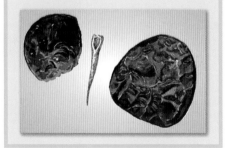

WHEN WAS BABYLON FOUNDED?

After the fall of Ur in 2000 BCE, many cities of Mesopotamia were ruled by the Amorites, whose two strongholds were Isin and Larsa. In 1763 BCE, Larsa fell to a great army led by Hammurabi (1792–1750 BCE). The new ruler gave a new name to the kingdoms of Sumer and Akkad – Babylonia.

The city of Babylon had magnificent temples and palaces. People entered the city through eight great bronze gates. The most magnificent of these was the Ishtar Gate, which was decorated with patterns and pictures of lions, bulls and dragons – all in shiny, patterned bricks.

Babylon's winding, narrow streets were lined with private houses. Most of the houses had a courtyard with rooms around it. In the city walls were gates, around which traders held markets. Traders and merchants travelled as far afield as Syria, Assyria and the kingdoms of the Persian Gulf.

The Ishtar Gate

FACT FILE

The Babylonians produced written records by carving picture symbols onto clay tablets. The tablets carried information about astronomy and mathematics, as well as records of legal and business matters and religious texts.

?

DID YOU KNOW THAT THE ANCIENT BABYLONIANS WERE THE FIRST TO STUDY THE STARS, SOME TIME BEFORE 2000 BCE? THEY KNEW OF FIVE PLANETS: JUPITER, MARS, MERCURY, SATURN AND VENUS.

WHERE ARE THE RUINS OF PERSEPOLIS?

This ancient city was originally called Parsa – city of the Persians. It was later known as Persepolis, from the Greek *perses polis*, which means 'Persian city'.

Persepolis was a capital of ancient Persia. King Darius I of Persia built Persepolis in about 500 BCE in a mountain region of what is now southwest Iran. Darius and his successors constructed large stone and mud-brick palaces in the capital, which became the royal ceremonial area for the religious holiday of the New Year. Every year at this festival, the king would renew his divine rights as king, and representatives of all the peoples within the Persian Empire would bring him gifts. In 330 BCE, Alexander the Great seized Persepolis.

Archaeologists have uncovered many of the ruins of Persepolis. Some of these ruins have been restored. Visitors may see a representation of the procession of New Year's gift givers carved in stone on two grand staircases leading to the king's audience hall.

• FACT FILE •

Ten thousand soldiers called the Immortals formed the core of the Persian army. Each spearman or archer was instantly replaced if killed.

IN WHICH COUNTRY WAS ANCIENT CARTHAGE?

Carthage was on the Mediterranean coast of what is now Tunisia, on the eastern side of Lake Tunis. According to legend, it was founded by Queen Dido in 814 BCE as an outpost of the Phoenician Empire, which was based in Tyre (now in southern Lebanon). Over the following centuries it became dominant in the western Mediterranean but as the Roman Empire grew in strength, conflict became inevitable and Rome won all the three wars between them. In the first Punic War, Rome gained Sicily, then later annexed Sardinia and Corsica. In the second, Hannibal failed to regain territory while, in the third, Rome destroyed the city of Carthage and took over the Carthaginian empire.

• FACT FILE •

Thynes, a settlement on the site of present-day Tunis, was part of the ancient empire of Carthage. The settlement gradually developed into the city of Tunis.

DID YOU KNOW THAT HANNIBAL WAS A GREAT MILITARY COMMANDER OF THE ANCIENT WORLD? HE FOUGHT THE ROMANS, LOSING ONLY 4,000 MEN TO THEIR 50,000.

HOW WERE THE EGYPTIAN PYRAMIDS BUILT?

THE PYRAMID THAT IS CONSIDERED TO BE EGYPT'S EARLIEST IS CALLED THE PYRAMID OF DJOSER. IT WAS BUILT AROUND 4,650 YEARS AGO!

Pyramid building developed slowly in ancient Egypt. The first pyramids were simple structures called *mastabas*, which were platforms built over the tombs of important people. Over the years further levels were added, until a structure called a step pyramid was produced.

In later pyramids, like those at Giza, the steps were filled in to produce the iconic conical shape. Pyramids were vital in the burial rites of rulers, ensuring their smooth passage to the afterlife. The pyramid builders used complex mathematical calculations, a system of levers and a vast workforce of slave labour in their construction.

• FACT FILE •

Civilizations sprang up at similar times in different parts of the world. One very advanced civilization was in the Indus Valley, in modern Pakistan and India. The remains of Harappa have been excavated, revealing a large city, with multi-storeyed buildings and carefully laid-out streets.

WHY IS THE GREAT SPHINX SUCH A MYSTERY?

The Great Sphinx is a mysterious rock sculpture with a human head on the body of a lion. This was built near the pyramids, outside modern Cairo, but the exact reason why is unknown. Historians believe it is older than the pyramids themselves.

Religion played an important part in Egyptian life. The Egyptians believed in many gods and goddesses. Gods looked after every aspect of life. Every town and city had its own god, too. Temples were dedicated to a particular god or a dead pharaoh.

Pyramids are the oldest stone structures in the world. They were built as tombs, to keep the body of the dead king safe for eternity and perhaps to ease his passage to the heavens.

The Great Sphinx is carved from a single piece of limestone rock. It measures 73m (240ft) long and 20m (65½ft) high.

WHY DID
CAVE PAINTERS PAINT?

Bushman rock paintings in Kamberg, South Africa

SEVERAL CAVES IN FRANCE AND SPAIN HAVE CAVE PAINTINGS DATING BACK TO 15,000 YEARS AGO. ONE, THE COSQUER CAVE NEAR MARSEILLE, FRANCE, HAS PAINTINGS THOUGHT TO BE AT LEAST 27,000 YEARS OLD!

• FACT FILE •

Woolly mammoths were found painted on the walls of caves. As well as being an important source of meat, woolly mammoths provided skins for clothing and shelter. Their tusks were also carved into tools and ornaments.

Archaeologists have discovered wonderful paintings on the walls of caves in France and Spain, which were painted by our early ancestors, thousands of years ago. They depict animals such as bulls, horses and antelopes, using natural paints made from earth pigments and plant extracts. We cannot be certain why they were painted, but at both the sites, dots mapping the night sky were discovered, as well as paintings of animals. The paintings may have been records of the position and quantity of game in certain areas; messages to other hunters perhaps or they may have had religious or magical significance.

WHAT IS THE TERRACOTTA ARMY?

In China the powerful Qin dynasty came to power in the 3rd century BCE. They swiftly conquered their neighbours to make a large empire covering most of modern China. The Qin emperor Shi Huangdi standardized weights and measures and introduced a single form of currency. He is best remembered for ordering the Great Wall of China to be built, but very little of this original wall now remains.

When the emperor died a huge tomb was built to hold his body. It was filled with a guardian army of thousands of life-sized terracotta warriors. The figures were placed in three pits inside the large complex surrounding the emperor's tomb.

 THERE ARE THOUGHT TO BE MORE THAN 8,000 SOLDIERS IN THE TERRACOTTA ARMY – NO TWO OF THEM ALIKE. EACH ONE OF THEM HAS TOTALLY UNIQUE FEATURES!

• FACT FILE •

The Chinese so much admired the swift horses of the central Asian steppes that they made more than 650 terracotta statues of them.

WHO BUILT THE PARTHENON?

The Parthenon was built by the ancient Greeks. Pioneers in medicine, mathematics and science, the ancient Greeks looked at the world in the light of logic and reason, and made some fundamental discoveries.

They built the Parthenon in Athens in the year 432 BCE, to venerate the city's protector, the goddess Athena. Her gold and ivory decorated statue was inside the great hall, enclosed by columns, which supported the roof like a forest of stones.

The Greeks built many beautiful temples to their gods. Stone columns, like those used in the Parthenon, were a typical feature of many Greek buildings.

A Greek politician called Pericles is credited with founding the city of Athens. He gave the task of designing the Parthenon to a famous sculptor of the time, called Phidias.

FACT FILE

Greek actors wore masks to show what kind of characters (comic or tragic) they played. Audiences would sit in the open air on a hillside to watch the plays.

WHY WAS THE GREAT WALL OF CHINA BUILT?

The Great Wall of China, at 6,400km (4,000 miles) is the longest structure in history and was built entirely by hand, under the direction of the government of the Ming dynasty (1368–1644) to protect China's borders from the threat of a Mongol invasion. The wall crosses northern China between the east coast and north-central China.

Most of what remains and is now known as the Great Wall dates from the late 15th century. The government believed that a fortified wall could act as a defence against incursions from their hostile neighbours. Although it is an outstanding achievement, it would never have protected China from a concerted and major attack. The Great Wall of China remains one of the modern wonders of the world.

Other wonders of the modern world include Machu Picchu in Peru, the Taj Mahal in India and the Colosseum in Rome.

WHEN WAS
HADRIAN'S WALL BUILT?

Hadrian's Wall was built in 122 CE to defend the northern frontier of Roman Britain. It acted as a checkpoint on movement between England and Scotland. At this time the Roman Empire was governed by the personal will of the emperor, but the emperor's power rested on his army. Weak or bad emperors were sometimes overthrown by army generals. Some emperors ruled well – Hadrian, for example, travelled widely to inspect building projects. Others, such as Nero and Caligula, were cruel or mad. The Romans were such good organizers that the empire usually kept working even when there was a fool at its heart.

 DID YOU KNOW THAT THE WALL TOOK EIGHT YEARS TO BUILD AND STRETCHES AS FAR AS 118KM (73 MILES)?

• FACT FILE •

A Roman coin stamped with the head of the Emperor Hadrian. During his reign, Hadrian personally visited nearly every province in the Roman Empire.

WHO BUILT THE
HAGIA SOFIA IN ISTANBUL?

The Hagia Sofia mosque in Istanbul was built by Byzantine Emperor Justinian I in around 500 CE. It can be found in Sultanahmet, the historical core to the south of the city, along with the Topkapi Palace, the Blue Mosque and the 4,000 shops of the covered bazaar. Istanbul is the largest city in Turkey and lies to either side of the Bosphorus – between the Sea of Marmara and the Black Sea. The Golden Horn is an inlet to the west of this strait. The Golden Horn was an important harbour and twice during the city's long history, its capture led to the fall of the city. The building of the Hagia Sofia mosque was part of a large-scale building programme instigated by Justinian I during a time when the Byzantine Empire was flourishing.

?

DID YOU KNOW THAT THE HAGIA SOFIA WAS ORIGINALLY A CHRISTIAN CHURCH? IT SERVED AS A CATHEDRAL UNTIL 1453, WHEN THE OTTOMAN SULTAN MEHMED II CONQUERED ISTANBUL AND CONVERTED THE BUILDING INTO A MOSQUE.

WHAT IS SUTTON HOO?

Replica of the decorated gold and silver Saxon helmet found at Sutton Hoo

The most powerful ruler among Anglo-Saxon kings was acknowledged as 'Bretwalda', or supreme king. The Sutton Hoo ship burial site in Suffolk was discovered in 1939. It is almost certainly the monument to King Redwald of East Anglia, who was Bretwalda in the 620s CE, and who died in 627 CE.

Artefacts unearthed by archaeologists at the Sutton Hoo site included a gold belt, a sword and a shield. There were also several items of jewellery. Most importantly there was a sceptre and standard, which must have belonged to the dead King Redwald himself. The iron helmet pictured was another one of the treasures unearthed at Sutton Hoo.

The Anglo-Saxons were made up of various peoples, including Angles, Saxons, Jutes and Frisians. During the 7th century they were in control of most of southern England.

WHERE DID WILLIAM THE CONQUEROR BUILD NORMAN CASTLES?

The introduction of castles to England followed the Norman Conquest of 1066. In fact, castles were the means by which William the Conqueror and his followers secured their hold on England following their victory at the Battle of Hastings.

William ordered castles to be built at Warwick, Nottingham, York, Lincoln, Cambridge and Huntingdon. These defensive structures helped to secure his newly acquired lands.

The first Norman castles were hurriedly constructed of earth and timber. Conwy Castle in north Wales is typical of the castles built by the Normans to withstand a long siege. Windsor Castle, Berkshire, is perhaps England's most famous castle.

Conwy Castle in Wales

• FACT FILE •

The Bayeux Tapestry was made by the Normans to celebrate their victory over the English in 1066. It is a huge series of pictures depicting incidents during the Norman Conquest.

William the Conqueror was the first Norman king of England, crowned in Westminster Abbey on Christmas Day in 1066.

WHO BUILT BEIJING'S FORBIDDEN CITY?

The first Ming emperor, Chu Yuan-Chang, turned Beijing into one of the greatest cities in the world, with the Forbidden City at its core. The Forbidden City and the Imperial City lie within the Inner City, an area in Beijing, the capital of China. The Forbidden City includes palaces of former Chinese emperors. It was so named because only the emperor's household was allowed to enter it. The buildings in this part of Beijing are now preserved as museums. The Imperial City surrounds the Forbidden City. The city includes lakes, parks and the residences of China's communist leaders.

• FACT FILE •

The roofs of these gates are supported on brackets – a typical feature of Chinese imperial architecture.

DID YOU KNOW THAT YELLOW WAS THE OFFICIAL COLOUR OF THE CHINESE EMPERORS? ALMOST 90 PER CENT OF THE BUILDINGS IN THE FORBIDDEN CITY WERE GLAZED WITH YELLOW TILES.

WHICH CITY IS MOST ASSOCIATED WITH THE RENAISSANCE?

Florence, in Italy, is the city most associated with the Renaissance. Meaning 'rebirth' the Renaissance was a 14th- to 17th-century period of political, artistic, scientific, cultural, literary and social rebirth, especially in classical studies such as mathematics, astronomy, architecture and philosophy.

The movement spread from Florence throughout Italy and then into western Europe. It is thought that the patronage of wealthy and powerful families like the Medici in Florence, and the arrival of scholars and classical texts from Greece, following the collapse of the Ottoman Empire, may have been catalysts for this intense, wide-reaching creativity.

A column designed by Andrea Palladio, one of the great Renaissance architects. His buildings were designed using classical ideas.

Some of the best-known Renaissance artists are Michelangelo, Leonardo da Vinci, Tintoretto, Titian and Raphael.

WHY WAS THE PALACE OF VERSAILLES BUILT?

In the 17th century, Louis XIV of France was famous for his power and wealth. He was the most important monarch in Europe. The palace that was built for him at Versailles, outside Paris, became the model for palaces throughout the continent.

The palace took 47 years to build and was renowned for its extreme grandeur. Great crystal chandeliers hung from the ceilings, their candlelight reflected in gilded mirrors. Fine tapestries and paintings decorated the walls.

FACT FILE

There were more than 200 servants at Versailles and every minute of Louis XIV's day was organized to the last detail. There was even a duty to empty the king's chamber pot!

WHO BUILT
THE TAJ MAHAL?

Inside the Taj Mahal – all red stone and exquisite carving

Shah Jahan built the Taj Mahal as a mausoleum for his favourite wife, Arjumand Banu Begum, better known as Mumtaz Mahal ('Elect of the Palace'), who died shortly after giving birth to her 14th child, in 1631. Shah Jahan (1592–1666) was the fifth ruler of the Mughal Empire in India. During his reign, which began in 1628, the Mughals reached their artistic peak, with vast treasures and magnificent architecture. Shah Jahan also built a palace of great beauty in Delhi. These, and other buildings, still stand as examples of Mughal achievement. The Mughal dynasty began its decline because too much money was spent on luxuries and too much effort was wasted in war. Shah Jahan's reign was a troubled one, and one of his sons eventually took his throne by force.

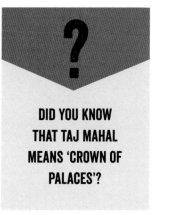

DID YOU KNOW THAT TAJ MAHAL MEANS 'CROWN OF PALACES'?

• FACT FILE •

A minaret, or tower, rises from each corner of the Taj Mahal. The Taj itself soars another 60m (196ft) into the air.

WHO BUILT
THE WINTER PALACE?

The Winter Palace is in St Petersburg, in northwestern Russia, near the mouth of the Neva River, on the Gulf of Finland. At the time it was built, St Petersburg was the imperial capital of the Russian Empire, and the Tsars and their courtiers built many palaces here. The Winter Palace was designed by Bartolomeo Rastrelli in a Baroque fashion, and was built between 1754 and 1762, during the reign of Empress Elizabeth, but the first royal resident was Catherine the Great. The palace, which suffered a major fire in 1837 but was beautifully rebuilt, now holds part of the collections of the State Hermitage Museum, has 1,057 halls and rooms, 1,786 doors and 1,945 windows.

DID YOU KNOW THAT THE WINTER PALACE HAS BEEN PAINTED VARIOUS DIFFERENT COLOURS? TODAY IS IT PAINTED GREEN WITH WHITE ORNAMENTAL FEATURES, BUT IT HAS ALSO BEEN A SANDY YELLOW AND A DEEP RED COLOUR IN THE PAST.

WHO BUILT THE SUEZ CANAL?

The idea of a canal linking the Mediterranean to the Red Sea dates back to ancient times. It was Napoleon's engineers who, in around 1800, revived the idea of a shorter route to India via the Suez Canal. It was not until 1859 that Egyptian workers started working on the construction of the canal in conditions, described by historians, as slave labour.

The project was completed around 1867. Although Britain had played no part in building the Suez Canal in Egypt, it benefited greatly when it opened. The new 190km (118 mile) waterway shortened the route from Britain to India by around 9,700km (6,000 miles), thereby extending their powers of trading.

IT IS POSSIBLE THAT THE ANCIENT EGYPTIANS MAY HAVE TRIED BUILDING A CANAL THOUSANDS OF YEARS BEFORE THIS ONE, CONNECTING THE RED SEA TO THE RIVER NILE!

FACT FILE

The British queen, Victoria, was on the throne when work on the Suez Canal was first started, and when it opened. During her reign, which lasted 63 years, Britain's empire expanded greatly.

IN WHICH CITY WOULD YOU FIND BIG BEN?

You'll find Big Ben in London, the capital city of England. It is one of the country's most famous landmarks. Most people think Big Ben is a tower, but actually it is the name of the largest bell in the Elizabeth Tower of the Palace of Westminster, where the United Kingdom's Houses of Parliament sit. The Palace of Westminster was rebuilt after a fire destroyed almost all of its predecessor in 1834. The clock was installed in 1854 and the tower was finished in 1858. When the original 14.5-tonne (16-ton) bell was tested, it broke in half and had to be recast as a 12.5-tonne (13.7 ton) bell, which, although cracked, is still in use today. If it were not for all London's traffic noise, the bell could be heard chiming as far as 15km (9 miles) away.

• FACT FILE •

Some clocks register time on a 24-hour basis. On such a clock, 9 a.m. would be shown as 09:00 and 3 p.m. would be 15:00. This system avoids confusion between the morning and evening hours. The radio clock shown here says the time is 6.45 p.m.

DID YOU KNOW THAT THE TOWER HOUSING BIG BEN HAS HAD VARIOUS NAMES IN THE PAST, INCLUDING CLOCK TOWER AND ST STEPHEN'S TOWER?

IN WHICH CITY WOULD YOU FIND LIBERTY ISLAND?

THE STATUE OF LIBERTY IS MADE OF PLATES OF COPPER ON A STEEL FRAME. IT MEASURES 46M (151 FT) TALL AND WEIGHS A MASSIVE 185 TONNES (204 TONS).

Liberty Island is in New York Harbor, near Manhattan Island. It is known all over the world because it is the site of the Statue of Liberty, which was designed by Frédéric Auguste Bartholdi and built by Gustav Eiffel in the 1880s as a present from the French people to commemorate the United States' Declaration of Independence a century before. The statue stands in the remains of Fort Wood, an early 19th-century fort. The fort was declared a national monument in 1924, and the rest of the island was included in the monument in 1937. The Statue of Liberty overlooks Ellis Island, which was the main point of immigration for hundreds of thousands of people from Europe and Africa during the 19th and early 20th centuries. The statue's full title is Liberty Enlightens the World, reflecting the long-held American belief that they should be an example and a force for good in the world.

• FACT FILE •

The people of France gave the Statue of Liberty to the people of the United States in 1884. This gift was an expression of their friendship and of the ideal of liberty shared by the two countries.

EMPIRES, DYNASTIES, KINGDOMS

CONTENTS

WHERE DID SARGON OF AKKAD BUILD HIS EMPIRE?

Sargon of Akkad was a king who founded the first great empire in history. He built his empire in Mesopotamia (now mostly Iraq) in about 2300 BCE and gained control over much of southwestern Asia. Sargon was an outstanding military leader and administrator. He was one of the earliest kings to maintain a permanent army and to appoint associates from the royal court to serve as the governors of conquered cities. He organized his empire so well that it survived under his successors for over 60 years. Sargon started his political career as cup-bearer to the king of Kish. Sargon later conquered Kish and the other Sumerian city states. Then he led his soldiers to a series of victories that extended his empire to what is now Iran in the east and to the Mediterranean Sea and Asia Minor (now Turkey) in the west.

King Sargon reigned for 56 years and built a magnificent capital city called Akkad.

FACT FILE

Sargon made one of his daughters a priestess of the Moon god in Ur. The royal standard of Ur, a decorated wooden box, dates from about 2500 BC. On its mosaic panels, farmers parade and soldiers march into battle.

WHICH DYNASTY WAS THE FIRST TO RULE CHINA?

The Shang dynasty was the earliest known Chinese ruling family. The dynasty governed from about 1766 BCE to around 1122 BCE. Its centre was in what is now known as the northern Henan Province. Shang society, though based on agriculture, became famous for its fine carvings and bronze work. Most Shang relics found by archaeologists come from Anyang, a city with houses, palaces, temples and elaborate tombs.

The people of the Shang period used bronze to make vessels, weapons and chariot fixtures. They also carved marble and jade and wove silk into fine fabrics. The Shang kings were superstitious and consulted 'oracle bones' before making any important decisions.

• FACT FILE •

The Shang writing system had more than 3,000 symbols. It appears on pieces of bone, silk and even turtle shells.

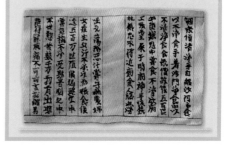

There were 30 Shang emperors in total. The first, a military leader, was called Tang Shang.

WHY WAS PERSIA A WELL-ORGANIZED EMPIRE?

Persia grew from the rubble of the defeated Assyrian Empire. In 612 BCE Nineveh, the Assyrian capital, fell. This left Babylon and Media to wrestle over the remains of the empire. In 550 BCE the Persian king Cyrus defeated the Medes and made himself ruler of a new empire.

Darius I ruled Persia from 521 to 486 BCE. He was a very able administrator. He organized the empire into provinces, each governed by a *satrap*. A *satrap* was like a king, but not as powerful as the emperor himself whose word was final. Darius encouraged trade through the use of coins and new canals. He and his son, Xerxes, tried to bring Greece within their empire, but failed. However Persia stayed rich and powerful until 331 BCE, when it was conquered by Alexander the Great.

The Persians were good fighters with cavalry and iron weapons, and their military energy proved too strong for their neighbours.

FACT FILE

The Persian Empire stretched from North Africa as far as the Caucasus Mountains in the north, and the borders of India in the east.

WHAT WAS THE BYZANTINE EMPIRE?

The Byzantines were renowned for their beautiful mosaics

The Roman Empire split in two in 395 CE. After the collapse of the western half in 476 CE, the eastern part survived. Its capital was called Byzantium, a city founded by the Greeks. The Roman emperor Constantine gave the city of Byzantium a new name, which was Constantinople.

The Byzantine Empire swallowed up Turkey, the Balkans, parts of Spain and North Africa, Egypt and the western coasts of the Mediterranean. The Empire was at its height under the rule of the 19th-century emperor Justinian and his influential wife Theodora. Through war and diplomacy, Justinian made Byzantium the greatest power in the eastern Mediterranean.

FACT FILE

Byzantine traders used gold coins called bezants. These coins have been found as far east as China and as far west as the British Isles.

?

DID YOU KNOW THAT BYZANTIUM, WHICH WAS LATER CALLED CONSTANTINOPLE, IS NOW THE MODERN CITY OF ISTANBUL?

WHAT WAS THE EXTENT OF THE ROMAN EMPIRE?

Rome grew from a small kingdom in Italy. It became a republic and one of the mightiest empires of the ancient world, with an empire stretching the length of the Mediterranean Sea. At its peak, the Roman Empire stretched from Britain in the west to Mesopotamia in the east. The army defended this empire well.

Rome rose to power thanks to its fertile farmland, its army and its key position in the middle of Italy. As well as fighting, Roman soldiers built roads, forts and aqueducts. Most people accepted Roman rule without question, because of the benefits it brought, letting them farm and trade in peace.

Pont du Gard, a Roman aqueduct in France

THE ROMAN EMPIRE WAS FOUNDED IN 27 BCE AND LASTED UNTIL 1453, WHEN IT WAS EVENTUALLY DISSOLVED. AT ITS PEAK, IT IS THOUGHT TO HAVE HAD A POPULATION OF AT LEAST 70 MILLION PEOPLE!

• FACT FILE •

Slaves made up about one-third of Rome's population. The slaves seen here are modern-day enthusiasts taking part in a gladiatorial show in Merida's amphitheatre, Spain. They carry the gladiators awards.

WHY WERE THE MONGOLS SO FEARED?

Genghis Khan was a Mongol warrior whose conquests built the greatest land empire in history. His vast empire stretched across central Asia from the Sea of Japan to the Caspian Sea and occupyied most of modern Russia.

The Mongols succeeded against established armies because they were unpredictable. They charged into battle on horseback, relying entirely on speed and surprise, and taking no prisoners. The Mongols were remorseless fighters, developing fighting machines that enabled them to break into the cities they besieged.

They were merciless towards those people who resisted them and sometimes they slaughtered entire populations. Most cities surrendered immediately, rather than risk being massacred!

• FACT FILE •

Marco Polo was one of the first Europeans to travel through Mongol territory. His reports helped to establish trade routes there.

WHY WAS FUJIWARA JAPAN A STRONG EMPIRE?

Prince Shotoku ruled Japan from 593 to 622 CE, strongly encouraged by Chinese ways. Shotoku believed that the Japanese emperor should be all-powerful, like the ruler of China. In 858 CE, however, the emperor lost control to a strong noble family called the Fujiwaras. The Fujiwaras had built up their power in the countryside, where they owned huge estates. Other nobles, too, had built up small 'empires' of their own.

The Fujiwaras gradually won control of the emperors, and of government, by marrying their daughters into the imperial family. The Fujiwaras held onto power in Japan for 300 years. During this time the great estates grew bigger and stronger, until the lords ruling over them were almost like kings.

The court of the Fujiwaras

FACT FILE

Japanese soldiers used iron swords and wore heavy armour. The bands of soldiers who served the land-owning lords became known as the samurai. They were the 'knights' of medieval Japan.

WHO WERE THE JAPANESE SHOGUNS?

Shogun was the title of the warrior rulers who led Japan from the late 12th century to the mid-19th century. The term *shogun* means 'great general' in Japanese. The emperor of Japan first gave this title to officers sent to fight tribes in the northern frontier region in the late 8th century. In 1192, the emperor gave the title shogun to the military leader Yoritomo of the Minamoto family. Yoritomo established a shogunate (warrior government) in Kamakura. The Kamakura shogunate, which lasted until 1333, shared civil and military rule with the imperial court at Kyoto.

The Ashikaga family established a shogunate in the Muromachi district of Kyoto in 1338. The Ashikaga shoguns were weak and unable to maintain control. This period was marked by battles among the warrior class, called the samurai. In 1603, clan leader Tokugawa Ieyasu defeated his rivals and established himself as shogun of the whole country.

• FACT FILE •

In 1603 Ieyasu founded the most powerful shogunate in Edo (now Tokyo). In 1867 the shogun resigned and returned power to the emperor.

SHOGUN IS SHORT FOR *SEI-I TAISHGUN*, WHICH TRANSLATES LITERALLY AS 'COMMANDER-IN-CHIEF OF THE EXPEDITIONARY FORCE AGAINST THE BARBARIANS'!

WHO WAS MANSA MUSA?

The mud mosque at Djenne. It stands on the site of an original, thought to have been built by Mansa Musa during the 13th century.

Mansa Musa was the founder of one of the wealthiest African empires in history – Mali. Starting in 1240, Musa built up his kingdom until it stretched for around 1,600km (995 miles) over West Africa. Much of the land was desert, but Mali grew rich from gold. Musa established an extensive programme of building in cities such as Timbuktu and Gao.

Very little is known about the early history of Africa. There must have been many great civilizations like Mali, but very few of them developed writing or left any records. Some civilizations built fine communities, such as the east coast port of Kilwa or the mysterious stone complex of Great Zimbabwe.

WHEN WAS THE BIGGEST GROWTH OF THE MUSLIM EMPIRE?

The advance of Islam seemed unstoppable in the late 600s CE. The Byzantine and Persian Empires could not halt the armies of Islam, and nor could Egypt. By 700 CE Muslims controlled most of the North African coast and ships patrolled the Mediterranean Sea and Indian Ocean. Muslims from Morocco invaded Spain, but the advance of Islam into western Europe was stopped in 732 CE by the Frankish army of Charles Martel.

Under the Ummayad family rule there were four classes of citizens: Arabian Muslims; new converts; Christians, Jews and Mandaens (a Persian sect); and slaves. The new converts included people from Egypt, Syria, Persia and Asia Minor. They adopted Arab ways, but brought to the Arabs a wealth of new learning in philosophy, medicine, art and science.

A scene from *The Thousand and One Nights*

WHY WAS THE TURKISH LEADER OSMAN SUCCESSFUL?

The Janissaries were members of an elite unit of soldiers and bodyguards that served the Ottoman Sultan from the end of the 15th century.

An Ottoman painting of a Janissary camp

In about 1300, a Turkish leader called Osman ruled a small kingdom in Anatolia (modern Turkey). His family name in Arabic was 'Othman', and is better known to us today as Ottoman.

Osman and his descendants were to build up one of the most important and long-lasting empires in world history. The Ottoman Turks started to take over parts of the weak Byzantine Empire. The new empire was a strong Muslim answer to the power of Christian Europe in the west.

In 1346 a Byzantine leader hired some Ottomon troops to fight for him, but this turned out to be a big mistake. It allowed the Ottomans to cross into Europe, thereby increasing their empire.

WHICH REGIONS WERE CONNECTED BY THE SILK ROAD?

The Silk Road was a group of ancient trade routes that connected China and Europe. The routes stretched across about 8,050km (5,000 miles) of mountains and deserts in central Asia and the Middle East between eastern China and the Mediterranean Sea.

The Silk Road got its name from the vast amount of Chinese silk carried along it. The cities along the Silk Road provided food, water and rest, as well as goods for trade. Of these cities, Khotan (now Hotan, China) was famous for its jade. The region of Fergana in present-day Uzbekistan was known for its powerful horses.

Camel caravans carried most goods across the dry, harsh regions along the Silk Road. By 800 CE, traffic began to decrease because traders started to travel by safer sea routes. A final period of heavy use occurred during the 13th and 14th centuries, when the Mongols ruled Central Asia and China.

Today, tourists can join a camel caravan treading the Silk Road path through the desert at Dunhuang City, China.

The Silk Road flourished primarily from 100 to 1500 CE.

• FACT FILE •

The Chinese were the first to learn how to make silk. They guarded their secret closely, and China was the only supplier of silk until the 6th century, when Western countries discovered how to make it.

WHEN DID THE GREAT NATIONS OF EUROPE EMERGE?

The great nations of Europe began to emerge after about 1450. For most of their history they had consisted of small warring states, or had been invaded by powerful neighbours. Now things were changing fast.

The connection between France and England was broken at last. Spain and Portugal grew stable enough to found their own great seagoing empires. Germany (part of the Holy Roman Empire) had strong leaders from the Habsburg dynasty.

The marriage in 1492 of King Ferdinand and Queen Isabella of Spain helped to unite the two strong Christian kingdoms of Aragon and Castile. Ferdinand and Isabella also completed the great 'reconquest' of Spain from Muslim control, which had begun over 400 years earlier.

A statue of the Catholic King Ferdinand and Queen Isabella in Plaza de los Reyes Católicos, Fuengirola, Spain.

FACT FILE

Unlike Spain, Italy remained a divided country, split up into several states ruled by different powers. In the north were the wealthy city-states, such as Florence, Milan and Urbino. Each ruling family had its own coat of arms.

WHY WAS THE REIGN OF ELIZABETH I SUCCESSFUL?

MORE THAN 200 PEOPLE WERE EXECUTED DURING ELIZABETH I'S REIGN. METHODS INCLUDED BEHEADING, BURNING AT THE STAKE AND BEING HUNG, DRAWN AND QUARTERED!

Elizabeth grew up in the political and religious turmoil of 16th-century England. Her mother, Anne Boleyn, was executed by her father when Elizabeth was only three, and she was imprisoned by her half-sister Queen Mary.

Elizabeth was highly intelligent, well-educated, purposeful and prudent, and strong-willed like her father Henry VIII. She had learned wisdom and caution from her experiences and she was appreciative of her devoted advisors. She realized that England needed prosperity, peace and stability. In 1559 she passed laws settling England's Protestant status and ended her reign as one of England's best-loved rulers.

• FACT FILE •

Elizabeth's signature on the death warrant of Mary Stuart. Elizabeth hesitated for days before signing it. She knew that Mary's death would give her Catholic enemies an excuse to attack her.

HOW DID THE SPANISH EMPIRE DEVELOP?

Hernán Cortés was a conquistador. This was the name given to a soldier or explorer who embarked on these overseas adventures.

A stone carving of the Aztec god known as Quetzalcoatl, Mexico

After the discovery of the Americas, Spanish adventurers set out to seek their fortunes. They sent expeditions to South and Central America and to Mexico in search of gold and treasure. In Mexico, a group of Spanish soldiers attacked the capital of the Aztec Empire. The Aztecs had been expecting the god Quetzalcoatl to return to Earth and believed that the leader of the raiders, Cortés, was this god. The Aztecs offered little resistance, so Cortés captured Montezuma, the Aztec emperor, and ruled in his place. In Peru, the adventurer Pizarro took advantage of a civil war to conquer the Incas, murdering their rulers.

Several factors made it easy for a small group of Spaniards to conquer these great civilizations. Though vastly outnumbered, the Spanish had horses, armour and guns, which gave them a huge advantage over the native warriors.

• FACT FILE •

Other nations expanded their empires in the same way as the Spanish. Many British people sailed to America to establish themselves and settle on this newly discovered land.

WHAT WAS THE EXTENT OF BRITAIN'S COLONIES IN THE 18TH CENTURY?

United Kingdom

Canada

India

Nigeria

■ British Empire
■ British Protectorates

South Africa

Commonwealth of Australia

THE BRITISH EMPIRE

The map to the left shows the extent of the empire in 1821.

Britain had started her collection of overseas colonies during the reign of Elizabeth I. By 1602, both England and the Netherlands had founded an 'East India Company' on the Indian coast to trade with the Far East.

The first settlements in North America took root and flourished in early Stuart times. In 1661, Britain gained her first African foothold, seizing James Island on the Gambia River. By the middle of the 1700s, these scattered colonies had begun to grow into a powerful and profitable empire. By the 1750s the British navy ruled the waves. By 1763 Britain had won most of France's territory in North America.

? DID YOU KNOW THAT BY 1924, THE BRITISH EMPIRE HAD GROWN SO LARGE THAT IT COVERED ONE-FIFTH OF ALL THE LAND IN THE WORLD?

• FACT FILE •

The British general, James Wolfe, brought French power in North America to an end. Wolfe's troops attacked and seized the town of Quebec. He died before the battle of Quebec ended.

REVOLUTION
AND WARFARE

CONTENTS

WHO WERE
THE HITTITES?

The Hittites were the earliest known inhabitants of modern-day Turkey. They began to rule the area in about 1900 BCE and during the next centuries, they conquered parts of Mesopotamia and Syria. By 1500 BCE, they had become a leading power in the Middle East. Hittite culture and language were Indo-European, but scholars do not know whether the Hittites came from Europe or from central Asia.

The Hittites were the first people to use chariots in war. Their archers fired arrows from these chariots, giving them a great advantage over enemies. One of the greatest battles of ancient times took place in about 1285 BCE at Kadesh on the Orontes River, north of Palestine. Mutwatallis, the Hittite leader, fought an indecisive battle against Egyptian forces under Rameses II.

THE BATTLE OF KADESH IS THOUGHT TO BE THE LARGEST CHARIOT BATTLE EVER FOUGHT. THE HITTITES ALONE HAD 3,500 CHARIOTS!

• FACT FILE •

This bronze sun disc originates from the Hatti civilization, which predates the Hittites by 300 years. It is likely that it was used during religious ceremonies.

WHERE WAS
THE BATTLE OF SALAMIS?

The Greeks trapped the Persian ships in the straits between mainland Greece and the island of Salamis and were able to attack them easily.

The Battle of Salamis took place on a Greek island of the same name, in the Saronic Gulf, about 16km (10 miles) west of Athens. It covers 95 sq km (37 square miles) and much of the land is rocky, mountainous and lacking in vegetation. Because the island has an irregular crescent shape, Salamis is known as Koulouri, which means 'baker's crescent'.

In 480 BCE the Greeks and Persians fought a great sea battle near Salamis. Arrows, stones and spears rained between the ships, but the Greek's key weapon was the ramming power of their galleys, driven at speed by banks of rowers. The Persian ships tried to block the advance of Greek vessels, but the Greeks still managed to destroy half of the Persian fleet.

• FACT FILE •

Broken pieces of pottery were used for letter-writing in the Greek world. Clay fragments are still found today.

WHY WERE ATHENS AND SPARTA RIVAL STATES?

Ancient Greek helmet

Ancient Spartan helmet

Athens was a rich and cultured state. Among its citizens were astronomers, mathematicians, thinkers, writers and artists. Although this was a society with slaves, the rulers had vision, and its government was the first real democracy.

Athens had the best navy in Greece while Sparta had the best army. Sparta's economy, like that of Athens, was based on slave workers, but there was no democracy as such.

Sport was encouraged, and girls as well as boys were expected to be fit and athletic. Sparta was run like an army camp, in which everyone was expected to obey.

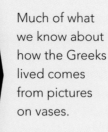

FACT FILE

Much of what we know about how the Greeks lived comes from pictures on vases.

? DID YOU KNOW THAT, IN SPARTA, BOYS AS YOUNG AS SEVEN WERE TAKEN FROM HOME AND TRAINED TO BE SOLDIERS?

WHY WAS THE ROMAN ARMY SO SUCCESSFUL?

The tortoise formation

THE ROMAN ARMY WAS MADE UP OF GROUPS OF 80 (CALLED CENTURIES) UNDER THE COMMAND OF ONE CENTURION. SIX CENTURIES FORMED A LARGER GROUP, CALLED A COHORT, AND TEN COHORTS MADE A LEGION – 4,800 IN TOTAL.

The Roman army invented a method of warfare that persisted for 2,000 years. Its troops were rigorously trained and exercised and divided into small detachments under the control of officers. Roman soldiers wore effective armour, and developed tactics that allowed them to fight successfully against almost any enemy. They were particularly good at defence. They used to close ranks and protect themselves with large shields, which deflected arrows and spears, until they reached close quarters and could use their own weapons. The group of soldiers shown above are in what was called the 'tortoise' formation, which proved to be impregnable against their Celtic foes.

• FACT FILE •

Emperor Trajan built a monument 30m (48ft) high to the Roman army. This section shows Roman legionnaires constructing a fort. These men were builders as well as fighters.

HOW SUCCESSFUL WERE VIKING ATTACKS?

The Vikings came from Scandinavia (the countries of Norway, Denmark and Sweden). Their homeland of mountains, fjords and forests offered little spare farmland for a growing population, so many Vikings went abroad in search of new lands to settle.

They were fierce warriors and their first impact on western Europe was a violent one. Norwegians and Danes began to sail across the North Sea in the late 700s CE, raiding the coasts of Britain and mainland Europe. They raided churches and towns, carrying off loot and took people as slaves. Their raids caused panic and rulers tried to buy off the invaders with gold. This only encouraged the Vikings to come back for more.

? DID YOU KNOW THAT, IN BRITAIN, THE VIKINGS WERE FINALLY DEFEATED BY ALFRED, THE KING OF WESSEX.

WHEN WAS THE NORMAN CONQUEST?

A scene from the Battle of Hastings

William of Normandy ruled England from 1066 to 1087. He claimed that Edward the Confessor promised him the throne in 1051. He also claimed that Harold (who was shipwrecked in France in 1064) had sworn to accept this.

The story of William's invasion and the Battle of Hastings on 14 October, 1066, is told in 72 woven scenes in the Bayeux Tapestry. After the crucial battle, William declared himself king. The English nobles lost their lands and French became the language of government. William and his barons built castles to guard their new land. A new age was beginning.

Ovingdean church, Sussex, is recorded in the Domesday Book.

?

DID YOU KNOW THAT THERE WAS A THIRD MAN CLAIMING THE ENGLISH THRONE AT THIS TIME? BEFORE MEETING WILLIAM THE CONQUEROR, HAROLD HAD TO DEFEAT THE VIKING HARALD HARDRADA, KING OF NORWAY, WHO CLAIMED TO BE A DESCENDANT OF KING CNUT, A FORMER ENGLISH KING.

HOW DID A SPIDER HELP ROBERT THE BRUCE?

Following the Battle at Bannockburn, the English king, Edward III, finally recognized the independence of Scotland and the right of Bruce to the throne, as King Robert I, in 1328.

A statue of Robert the Bruce at Bannockburn, Scotland

Robert the Bruce (1274–1329) was a gallant Scottish king. After claiming the throne in 1306, he spent most of his reign trying to free his country from English rule. A legend is told of Bruce hiding from his enemies. He was lying on a bed in a hut, when he saw a spider trying to swing itself from one beam to another by one of its threads. It tried six times and failed. Bruce realized that he had fought the same number of battles in vain against the English. He decided that if the spider tried a seventh time and succeeded, he would also try again. The spider's seventh attempt was successful, so Bruce took heart and went forth to victory.

Within two years he had gained control of almost all of Scotland. He then advanced into England, destroying everything in his path. In 1314, the English invaded Scotland, but Bruce's forces defeated them, in a battle at Bannockburn.

• FACT FILE •

Over 10,000 English soldiers were killed at the Battle of Bannockburn in 1314. By 1328 Bruce had driven the English out of Scotland.

WHEN WAS THE HUNDRED YEARS' WAR?

The 14th century was filled with wars. The longest and most exhausting of these was between England and France. It lasted, on and off, until the middle of the 1400s, and is known as the Hundred Years' War. It actually spanned from 1337 until 1453, by which time the French, inspired by Joan of Arc, had driven the English from Maine, Gascony and Normandy and the war was finally won.

The conflict was a very complicated one. The Plantagenet kings of England also ruled a large part of France, while the rest belonged to the king of France. Both kings wanted to be the sole ruler of a united country. There were plenty of other reasons for the war. The French supported the Scots in their struggle against England. The English, in turn, claimed the throne of France when Charles IV died in 1328 and left no heirs.

A significant battle for the English during this period was the Battle of Agincourt, fought in October 1415, and which the English won against all odds.

WHERE WAS THE BATTLE OF CRÉCY?

The Battle of Crécy was the first major battle of the Hundred Years' War (1337–1453) and fought at the site of the present village of Crécy, in France. The Hundred Years' War began in 1337 and continued for more than a century. It was not a single war, but rather a series of skirmishes between England and France. At Crécy, English troops under Edward III defeated a much larger French army under Philip VI. Almost half of the French force was killed in the Battle of Crécy, including more than a thousand knights. English archers on foot proved more effective than the armour-clad French knights on horses. The hero of the battle was Edward, the Black Prince, son of Edward III of England.

THE ENGLISH ARMY TOTALLED AROUND 13,000 MEN AGAINST A FRENCH ARMY OF 30,000– 40,000. IT WAS THE TACTICAL USE OF LONGBOW MEN THAT WON THE DAY FOR THE ENGLISH.

• FACT FILE •

Knights decorated their shield or standard with the heraldic symbols of their own coat of arms. This made it easier to identify the knight in full armour. Each coat of arms had its own unique design.

HOW WAS THE SPANISH ARMADA DEFEATED?

Sir Francis Drake was an English sea captain, privateer and navigator during the reign of English Queen Elizabeth I. He helped to defeat the Spanish Armada and was knighted by Elizabeth in 1581.

The English were envious of Spain's rich colonies in South and Central America. During the reign of Elizabeth I, the English raided Spanish ships carrying gold and silver to Spain. The Spanish suspected that the English Crown supported these privateers, which angered them. To make matters worse, an English army helped the Dutch who were fighting against Spanish rule. In 1588 Phillip of Spain sent the Spanish Armada to invade England. The Spanish came very close to actually conquering England at this time. Their Armada, however, was scattered by storms, then harried and destroyed by English ships.

WHY DID THE REFORMATION TAKE PLACE?

Luther at Wittenberg Castle

Martin Luther was a monk from Germany. In 1510 he visited Rome, the home of the Catholic Church, and was deeply shocked. He saw the Pope and his household living in great luxury, and realized the Church was bloated with wealth and power. Luther nailed his list of 95 arguments against the Church's sale of indulgences to the door of Wittenberg Castle in 1517. His ideas quickly spread across northern Europe. He begged the nobles of Germany to help him reform the old religion. This alarmed the Pope, who sent an order declaring that Luther was a heretic.

DID YOU KNOW THAT IT WAS MARTIN LUTHER WHO SPARKED THE SPLIT IN THE CHRISTIAN CHURCH THAT RESULTED IN TWO MAIN FACTIONS – THE CATHOLICS AND THE PROTESTANTS?

WHY DID THE THIRTY YEARS' WAR TAKE PLACE?

In 1619 the rebels expelled Ferdinand and chose a new king, the Protestant Frederick.

The struggle between Catholics and Protestants in Europe lasted for more than a century. It was made up of a series of great 'wars of religion', which involved countries as far apart as the Netherlands, Spain, Sweden, France and England. The last and biggest of these religious wars began where the Reformation itself had begun – in the bickering states of Germany. This messy conflict became known as the Thirty Years' War.

The war started in a dramatic way. Protestants in Bohemia were angry with their new king, Ferdinand. He wanted to restore Bohemia to the Catholic faith so he closed Protestant schools and ordered Protestant churches in Prague be pulled down. The Protestants banded together and threw some Catholic officials from an upstairs window in Prague Castle. This incident sparked off a civil war in Bohemia.

• FACT FILE •

When the Protestants threw the Catholic officials out of the window of Prague Castle, it became known as the 'Defenestration of Prague'.

WHO FOUGHT IN THE ENGLISH CIVIL WAR?

The English Civil War was fought between the Roundheads and the Cavaliers. In 1603, England had a new king – James I. He was the first of the Stuart monarchs and his accession to the English throne marked the end of the Tudor rule. James, son of Mary Queen of Scots, was already James VI of Scotland and wished to unite the kingdoms of the British Isles. His reign was very unpopular in England, but less so than that of his son Charles I, who came to the throne in 1625. Charles tried to rule without parliament and was faced with a rebellion. He tried, unsuccessfully to arrest five members of the House of Commons for treason, and was forced to flee to London. By August 1642 he had declared war on the parliamentary supporters (the 'Roundheads') and the civil war began.

It was Oliver Cromwell who led the Parliamentary forces to victory in the English Civil War. He went on to rule England from 1653–1658.

• FACT FILE •

Oliver Cromwell reorganized the Roundhead forces into a professional force known as the 'New Model Army'. King Charles I's men were known as the Cavaliers.

WHERE WAS BONNIE PRINCE CHARLIE'S REBELLION?

• FACT FILE •

Bonnie Prince Charlie did lead his army to victory over the English in 1745. He was born in Rome and spent the latter years of his life in Italy. His full name was Charles Edward Louis Philip Casimir Stuart.

Charles Edward Stuart (1720–1788) was also known as Bonnie Prince Charlie. He was the grandson of James II, and the last member of the Stuart family to try and claim the throne of England. In the late summer of 1745, Charles landed in Scotland. Many supporters joined his rebellion, especially among the Scottish clans in the north. Within weeks, he occupied Edinburgh. By early December he had marched as far south as Derby in England. But Charles found little support in England and retreated to Scotland. On April 16, 1746, his army suffered a devastating defeat at Culloden Moor, near Inverness. Charles then hid as a fugitive in the Scottish Highlands, until he sailed back to France in September.

WHEN WAS THE AMERICAN REVOLUTION?

The American victory over the British at Saratoga in 1777

The 13 American colonies were: Connecticut, Delaware, Georgia, Maryland, Massachusetts Bay, New York, New Hampshire, New Jersey, Pennsylvania, Rhode Island and Providence Plantations, North Carolina, South Carolina and Virgina.

By the year 1763 more than two million British colonists were living in North America. Their main ambition was to be able to govern themselves.

Britain, however, had different ideas about her colonies, because they were an important market for trade. The British government was concerned about who was going to pay for the British forces that were still stationed to protect North America. The answer was the colonists themselves through new and increased taxes.

The Americans had never been taxed before and protested loudly. They had no-one to put their case to the parliament in London, so they took direct action.

By 1775 the whole colony was in a state of rebellion. This was the opening of America's bitter struggle for freedom.

● FACT FILE ●

On July 4, 1776, representatives of the 13 colonies signed a Declaration of Independence. This broke off all political connections with Britain.

WHY DID THE BOSTON TEA PARTY TAKE PLACE?

THE THREE BRITISH SHIPS WERE CALLED *THE DARTMOUTH, THE BEAVER* AND *THE ELEANOR.* BETWEEN THEM THEY WERE CARRYING 342 CHESTS OF TEA – ALL THROWN OVERBOARD!

The British government imposed several new taxes, on things as different as official paper and molasses. The Americans protested against them. Some of the taxes were removed, but import duties on luxury goods such as tea were increased instead.

With no one to fight their case, the American people decided to take action. In 1773, a band of colonists seized three British ships in Boston harbour, Massachusetts and dumped their cargo of tea overboard.

This event became known as the 'Boston Tea Party'. It enraged the British government so much that they sent troops to put Massachusetts under military rule.

FACT FILE

In 1775 George Washington was elected as commander-in-chief of the colonists' army. To many Americans at that time, he became a leading symbol of their fight for independence.

WHICH EVENT SPARKED THE FRENCH REVOLUTION?

The Bastille was a former fortress in Paris that was later used as a prison by French monarchs.

On 14 July 1789, a mob attacked the royal prison in Paris, the Bastille. Although only a few prisoners were released, this event marked the end of royal power in France and the beginning of the revolution.

During the 1700s France was not prosperous. The government was short of money and needed to raise taxes. Louis XVI could only do this by recalling a traditional assembly, which promptly demanded political reforms. He responded by trying to dismiss the assembly, but the citizens of Paris revolted in support of the assembly. The new National Assembly showed its strength by introducing fresh laws in 1791, insisting on freedom and equality. The royal family was imprisoned for a while, then tried and executed.

• FACT FILE •

During the French Revolution, a doctor and member of France's National Assembly, suggested the guillotine as an instrument of execution!

WHO FOUGHT AT THE BATTLE OF WATERLOO?

The Battle of Waterloo

Napoleon's distinctive hat

By 1812, Napoleon Bonaparte had created a French empire that covered almost the whole of Europe. However, after a disastrous campaign in Russia Napoleon's empire began to crumble. In April 1814, Napoleon was forced to abdicate. He went into exile in Elba, an island off the coast of Italy, only to return with fresh troops the following year to make another bid for power.

The combined armies of Britain, Austria, Prussia and Russia defeated Napoleon's army at the battle of Waterloo in 1815. It was to be Napoleon's last battle. The French had more soldiers and better artillery, but they were still soundly beaten. Napoleon was sent into exile on the island of St Helena, where he died in 1821.

Napoleon was a great military strategist, who seemed instinctively to know the best time to attack during battle.

• FACT FILE •

Napoleon's first wife was Josephine, the daughter of a planter from the French West Indies. She was both intelligent and beautiful, but she and Napoleon had no children.

WHEN DID WORLD WAR I BEGIN?

As the 19th century drew to a close, there was an increase in rivalry between the different nations of Europe. They competed against each other for control of colonies, and for industrial and military power. In 1882, Germany, Austria–Hungary and Italy (known as the Central Powers) formed an alliance called the Triple Alliance, promising to protect each other in the event of an attack. In 1904, Britain joined with France in a similar alliance. They were joined by Russia in 1907 to form the Triple Entente. Europe was finally plunged into war by the action of an assassin in the Bosnian city of Sarajevo in 1914. Soon all the major European powers were drawn into conflict. Russia, backed by France, supported Serbia. Then Germany invaded neutral Belgium and attacked France, drawing Britain into the conflict.

World War I trenches with sandbags

THE MEN SERVING AT THE FRONT DURING WORLD WAR I WERE STILL ABLE TO RECEIVE MAIL. DURING THE COURSE OF THE CONFLICT, AS MANY AS TWO BILLION LETTERS WERE DELIVERED!

• FACT FILE •

A British soldier from World War I. Typically, soldiers would spend a week or more in a front-line trench before going back to their dugout in a support trench.

WHICH MACHINES MADE THEIR DEBUT IN WORLD WAR I?

THE SOPWITH CAMEL WAS BRITAIN'S MOST SUCCESSFUL AIRCRAFT DURING THE CONFLICT. IT ENTERED THE WAR IN 1917 AND SHOT DOWN MORE ENEMY PLANES THAN ANY OTHER ALLIED AIRCRAFT!

World War I was the first mechanized war in history. In the beginning, fighting was similar to wars fought in the previous century. But new and terrifying weapons were introduced that completely changed the whole style of warfare. Aircraft were used for the first time to observe the enemy and to locate suitable targets for the long-range artillery. Later on, fighter planes began to shoot down the spotters, introducing aerial warfare.

Aircraft and Zeppelin airships were used as bombers. The most terrifying new weapon was poison gas, which was used by both sides. It caused millions of deaths and terrible suffering. Tanks also made their first appearance.

• FACT FILE •

World War I (1914–18) saw the first appearance of armoured tanks in battle. They were able to break through enemy lines and create openings for troops to advance through. Earlier use of tanks could have saved lives and helped shorten the war.

WHICH EVENT LED TO THE EASTER RISING?

Easter Monday 1916

Wartime prime minister, David Lloyd George, proposed that Ireland would stay under British control, but that the Irish Free State would become a British dominion.

In 1870, a movement calling for Home Rule was founded in Ireland. Supporters of Home Rule wanted a separate parliament to deal with Irish affairs in Dublin. The prime minister at the time, William Gladstone, was a staunch supporter of Home Rule, but he failed to get his Home Rule Bill approved by parliament.

During World War I, the issue of Home Rule continued to cause conflict in Ireland. When war actually broke out in 1914, most Irish Volunteers supported Britain in its fight against the Central Powers. But a breakaway group formed the Irish Republican Brotherhood (later known as the IRA). On Easter Monday, 1916, protesters belonging to this and other nationalist movements seized buildings in Dublin and proclaimed Ireland a republic. This rebellion became known as the Easter Rising.

• FACT FILE •

In this image, Irish politician Charles Parnell addresses an audience in support of Home Rule. He became leader of the Home Rule Party in the British parliament and fought tirelessly for his beliefs.

WHY DID THE USA ENTER THE WAR IN 1915?

• FACT FILE •

Poppies were in flower on many of the French battlefields of World War I. Today, artificial poppies are sold in Europe and the USA to raise money for war veterans.

From the start of the Great War, the name by which World War I was first known, British warships blockaded German ports. In this way Britain's navy prevented supplies from reaching Germany, causing severe shortages of food and other goods. The Germans retaliated with their submarines, called U-boats.

After 1915, U-boats attacked both warships and merchant shipping vessels carrying supplies to Britain. In May 1915, a German torpedo hit a British passenger ship called the *Lusitania*. The ship was carrying nearly 2,000 passengers, including many Americans. The sinking of the *Lusitania* was one of the factors that eventually drew the United States into the war.

?

DID YOU KNOW THAT, IN 1917, THE GERMANS SENT A TELEGRAM TO MEXICO, PERSUADING THEM TO DECLARE WAR ON THE USA IF THE AMERICANS ENTERED THE WAR? THE TELEGRAM WAS INTERCEPTED BY THE BRITISH AND NOTHING CAME OF IT.

WHEN WAS THE RUSSIAN REVOLUTION?

Nicholas II and his family were imprisoned by the Bolsheviks in 1917. They were most probably shot a year later.

The last tsar, Nicholas II, ruled from 1894 until his abdication in 1917. In the early years of his reign there was increasing discontent among ordinary Russians. Many people, including the Bolshevik leader Vladimir Illyich Lenin, followed the teachings of Karl Marx, the founder of communism. In 1905 this discontent boiled over when troops fired on thousands of striking workers outside the tsar's Winter Palace in St Petersburg. The rebellion was quickly put down, but hundreds of workers were killed and wounded.

In early 1917, riots broke out again and this time the troops supported the rioters. Nicholas II abdicated, and a provisional government was put in place.

• FACT FILE •

The hammer and sickle is a communist symbol that originated at the time of the Russian Revolution. The hammer represented factory workers and the sickle represented farm labourers.

HOW DID WORLD WAR II BEGIN?

WORLD WAR II KILLED MORE PEOPLE THAN ANY OTHER WAR IN HISTORY. SOME RECORDS CLAIM THAT OVER 60 MILLION PEOPLE DIED.

The bombed German city of Dresden

As in World War I, some international alliances were activated following the German invasion of Poland. As a result of this Britain and France declared war on Germany.

When the Germans attacked Poland, the Russians also attacked the country and it was divided. The Germans went on to invade Denmark, Norway, Belgium, the Netherlands and France in quick succession. They crushed any resistance with overwhelming armoured forces. The fighting spread to nearly every part of the world and included nearly 60 nations. The Americans entered the war in 1941 after being attacked by Germany's ally Japan. At this time a huge military build-up began in England.

• FACT FILE •

Britain was led through World War II by Winston Churchill. He is remembered for his great wartime leadership qualities. He is also remembered for his famous 'V for victory' sign.

WHO FOUGHT IN THE BATTLE OF BRITAIN?

During World War II, Britain and France became trapped by the rapid German invasion. In June 1940, the French signed a truce with Germany and Britain stood alone against the Germans. Italy joined the war, siding with the Germans. In June 1940 Hitler made plans to invade Britain.

However, he first needed to gain control of the skies. The Battle of Britain began in July 1940 between the German airforce, the Luftwaffe, and Britain's Royal Air Force (RAF). By May 1941 the RAF had gained the upper hand and Hitler stopped bombing Britain.

DID YOU KNOW THAT THE BATTLE OF BRITAIN WAS THE FIRST BATTLE IN HISTORY TO BE FOUGHT PRIMARILY IN THE AIR?

WHAT WAS
THE BLITZKRIEG?

Members of a German reenactment Panzer Group sit on their World War II Panzer IV.

'Blitzkrieg' or lightning war was a style of fighting introduced during World War II. This war was very different to the first international conflict. Trench warfare, which had claimed so many lives, was now an outdated concept. So it was that when Adolf Hitler invaded Poland in September 1939 he unleashed a new and frightening brand of warfare into the world – 'Blitzkrieg'. The key to the success of Blitzkrieg was the use of tanks in very large numbers and innovative style. The tanks charged ahead independent of the troops and wreaked havoc among defenders.

The idea behind the Blitzkrieg was to attack rapidly, catching the enemy unawares. That way they would be poorly equipped to defend themselves.

• FACT FILE •

World War I had deadly weaponry, too. Newly introduced machine guns changed trench warfare. Now soldiers could easily wipe out large numbers of the enemy.

WHY WERE THE D-DAY LANDINGS A TURNING POINT IN THE WAR?

A naval memorial for the battle of Utah Beach in Normandy, France, part of the D-Day landings.

In June 1944, the Allied leaders decided that it was time to attack Germany itself. Under the overall command of US General Eisenhower, Allied troops landed in Normandy and advanced across France. Meanwhile, Soviet troops moved across Eastern Europe.

On the morning of 6 June, 1944, thousands of Allied troops went ashore along the coast of Normandy in northern France in what became known as the D-Day landings.

Utah Beach was just one of five landing zones on a 80-km (50-mile) stretch of coastline. The others were codenamed Omaha, Gold, Sword and Juno.

FACT FILE

Charles de Gaulle was leader of the French troops, known as the Free French, who had escaped occupied France. After the war, he became one of the country's most powerful presidents ever.

WHEN WAS THE BOMBING OF PEARL HARBOR?

In August 1945, the United States effectively brought the war against Japan and, therefore, World War II to a catastrophic end when it dropped two atomic bombs on the Japanese cities of Nagasaki and Hiroshima. An estimated 130,000 people were killed and many more suffered terrible after-effects.

On 7 December, 1941, there was a surprise attack by the Japanese airforce on the United States navy base at Pearl Harbor in Hawaii. Although the attack crippled the US Navy in the Pacific Ocean, it also drew the Americans into World War II. The USA and its Allies declared war on Japan on 8 December, 1941. Japan joined Germany and Italy to form the Axis alliance. During the summer of 1942, US forces successfully halted the Japanese advance at the battles of Midway Island, Guadalcanal and Coral Sea. After Pearl Harbor, however, Japanese forces quickly took control of much of Southeast Asia, including Singapore, Burma and the Philippines.

ONE OF THE SHIPS TARGETED AT PEARL HARBOR WAS THE USS *ARIZONA*. HAVING REFUELLED THE PREVIOUS DAY, THE SHIP HAD 1.5 MILLION GALLONS OF OIL ON BOARD. ALTHOUGH MUCH OF THIS WAS BURNED DURING THE ATTACK, 500,000 GALLONS REMAINED AND CONTINUE TO LEAK INTO THE HARBOUR TO THIS DAY!

WHERE WAS THE BATTLE OF DIEN BIEN PHU?

Vietnam is a tropical country in Southeast Asia. China governed the area from about 100 BCE until 900 CE, when the Vietnamese established an independent state.

Fighting broke out between French forces and the Vietminh in 1946. It ended in 1954, with the French defeat at the Battle of Dien Bien Phu. An international conference to arrange a peace settlement also took place at this time.

In 1957, Vietminh members in the south of Vietnam began to rebel against the South Vietnamese government. Fighting broke out and it developed into the Vietnam War. The United States became the chief ally of the South.

French trenches at Dien Bien Phu, Vietnam

Unable to overcome the North Vietnamese and their allies, the American forces withdrew from Vietnam in 1973.

• FACT FILE •

The Vietnam War showed, for the first time, how a small country like North Vietnam could take on, and eventually defeat, the military might of the United States, by using superior tactics.

WHAT WAS THE CUBAN MISSILE CRISIS?

In 1949, the Western Allies formed the North Atlantic Treaty Organization (NATO) for defence against the communist presence in Europe. In the same year, the USSR exploded its first atomic bomb. With both superpowers holding nuclear weapons, fear and mistrust between the two sides increased.

The Soviets constructed a wall across Berlin in 1961, separating East from West in the city. In 1962, the Cuban crisis erupted when the USA discovered that the USSR was building missile sites on the island of Cuba in the Caribbean. These sites were within range to launch an attack by nuclear weapons on American cities. The two superpowers came to the brink of war before the USSR agreed to withdraw the weapons. Although the two superpowers never became involved in direct warfare, both sides became involved in wars elsewhere in the world. The USA fought communism and the USSR helped communist fighters.

• FACT FILE •

John Fitzgerald Kennedy, pictured here on a stamp, was US president from 1961 until he was assassinated in 1963. During his presidency the Berlin Wall was built, dividing the city in two and stopping East Germans escaping communist rule.

JOHN F. KENNEDY

13c UNITED STATES

RELIGION
AND IDEOLOGY

CONTENTS

WHY DID THE EGYPTIANS MAKE MUMMIES?

The Egyptians believed in an afterlife to which human souls journeyed after death. They thought it important that the bodies of the dead should be preserved for life in the next world, and so they developed techniques for making 'mummies'. The dead person's organs were removed and the body was embalmed and dried, using salts and chemicals, and then wrapped in linen bandages. It was then placed inside a coffin. Even animals such as cats and monkeys were sometimes mummified. Many thousands of mummies must have been made, but only about 1,000 of them survive today.

Tutankhamen became king of Egypt at the age of nine and died when he was about 18. His tomb is one of more than 60 royal tombs around the Valley of the Kings. Its four rooms contained more than 5,000 objects, which included ostrich feathers, model ships, a throne and a gold death mask.

Tutankhamen's burial mask

THE ANCIENT EGYPTIANS USED TO REMOVE THE BRAIN PRIOR TO MUMMIFICATION, OFTEN SUCKING THE ORGAN OUT THROUGH THE NASAL PASSAGES!

WHO DID THE PERSIANS WORSHIP?

The Persians did not build temples but worshipped on the mountaintops.

The Persians believed in gods of nature, such as the Sun and the Sky, thinking that they had special powers. Mithras, the god of light, can be seen above, killing a bull as a sacrifice to renew life.

Zoroaster (Zarathustra) was a prophet who lived sometime between 628 and 551 BCE. He reformed the ancient religion and many people followed his teachings. He taught that life is a struggle between the truth and the lie and that the purpose of humankind is to maintain truth. He preached good thoughts, words and deeds and introduced the concept of free will. He emphasized a supreme god, Ahura Mazda, 'the wise spirit', a winged god of light, who became chief god throughout Persia.

• FACT FILE •

Darius I ruled Persia from 521 to 486 BCE and is depicted here in a Roman mosaic. He encouraged trade through the use of coins and new canals. Darius sent an army into Greece in 490 BCE, but it was defeated by Athenian forces at Marathon. Darius died in 486 BCE while preparing for new attacks on Greece.

WHO DID THE ANCIENT GREEKS WORSHIP?

The life of the ancient Greeks was ruled by a hierarchy of gods and goddesses, present in all of nature and deeply involved in, and influencing, the life of humanity. The Greeks believed that the Universe was a sphere. The upper half was light and airy, the lower half dark and gloomy, and the Earth a flat disc, floating between the two.

Zeus

The most important gods, led by Zeus, lived on Mount Olympus and the first Olympic games (776 BCE) were held in his honour. The underworld, where people went after death, was the realm of Hades, and the sea was ruled by Poseidon, the brothers of Zeus. All three held power over the Earth. The three brothers were believed to have defeated the Titans to become masters of the Universe.

Poseidon

FACT FILE

The ruins of Greek and Roman temples can be seen across Europe, the Near East and North Africa. Every town had its own temple, dedicated to a god or goddess.

WHO WAS PAN?

According to an ancient Greek myth, Pan was a god who invented the first musical instrument – the pipes that are named after him – after he accidentally breathed through old reeds beside a river and produced a wail. He so liked the sound that he broke the reeds off and tied them together. The reeds were different lengths and produced varied notes.

The first musical instruments were probably drums, made of hollow logs, and sticks that were hit together to provide a beat for dancing. Animal horns were later used to make simple wind instruments and early stringed instruments include the lyre, in which strings are strung from a simple frame and plucked.

Another Greek god was Eros, god of love. He was a winged god armed with a bow and a quiver of arrows, which he aimed at couples to make them fall in love.

WHERE DID THE GREAT RELIGIONS OF THE WORLD BEGIN?

The great religions of the world all began in Asia. Three of them – Judaism, Christianity and Islam – began in the same area of west Asia. Hinduism and Buddhism began in India. People all over the world formed systems of beliefs in powers greater than their own.

The earliest religions were connected with the forces of nature – the Sun, the Moon, wind, water, rocks and trees – and with animals. Hinduism is the oldest of the Asian beliefs. There are many Hindu gods and rules governing foods, conduct, festivals and even the jobs that people do. Hindu sculptures of gods and goddesses are full of energy. The four-armed Vishnu is the preserver of the Universe. He is one of Hinduism's two main gods – the other is Shiva.

Buddhism began in India in about 500 BCE, and was later spread by missionaries to Burma and China.

Four-armed Vishnu

A bronze statue of the Buddha

WHY DID THE ROMANS PERSECUTE CHRISTIANS?

The Sermon on the Mount

The teachings of Jesus were spread widely by his followers after his death. At first, the Christians were ignored by the Romans, especially as they did not join in the Jewish rebellion against Roman rule in 66 CE. However, the early Christians began to travel around the Roman Empire, and when they reached Rome they began to recruit new followers. The Roman authorities became concerned that this new religion would threaten the established order.

The ancient Romans did not object to the new religion itself, but they did object to the fact that it denied the emperor's divinity. The new religion appealed to the poor and to the slaves, and its popularity was seen as a threat to Roman society.

THE CHRISTIANS WERE PERSECUTED BY THE EMPEROR NERO, WHO ORDERED FOR THEM TO BE SET UPON BY SAVAGE DOGS OR BURNT ALIVE.

• FACT FILE •

The symbol of a fish was used by the early Christians in Rome as a secret symbol to identify themselves to other Christians. The symbol was simple and quick to draw. It was not likely to be noticed by the Romans.

WHY WERE THE
DEAD SEA SCROLLS HIDDEN?

The Dead Sea Scrolls are religious writings that were first discovered in 1947, hidden in caves near the Dead Sea. The dry atmosphere of the caves had the effect of preserving the scrolls. About 800 scrolls have been found, mostly in a place called Qumran in Israel. They date from between 150 BCE and 68 CE, and they include all of the books of the Old Testament except for Esther.

Scholars believe that the scrolls were concealed by members of a religious sect called the Essenes, who lived in the isolated community. They hid the scrolls to keep them safe during political unrest in the area, and they remained hidden for hundreds of years.

The Museum of Israel, Jerusalem, which houses the Dead Sea Scrolls

SCHOLARS BELIEVE THEY HAVE FOUND THE REMAINS OF AROUND 850 SEPARATE SCROLLS!

• FACT FILE •

The Dead Sea Scrolls are ancient documents written on leather and copper.

WHY DOES JERICHO HAVE A PLACE IN JEWISH HISTORY?

The Bible records that Abraham had two sons, Ishmael (the ancestor of the Arabs) and Isaac. Isaac had two sons, Esau and Jacob, and Jacob (also called Israel) had 12 sons. These sons became the heads of the Twelve Tribes, the Israelites of the Bible.

The Israelites became very wealthy and powerful people. Perhaps they are remembered best for their conquering of the city of Jericho. At God's command the walls of Jericho tumbled down at the sound of the Israelite army shouting and banging their drums.

Jericho is still a thriving city today, not far from the river Jordan in the West Bank.

• FACT FILE •

Solomon was the son of David, an Israelite king who ruled from 1010 to 970 BCE. David defeated the Philistines and enlarged the kingdom, making Jerusalem its capital city. Solomon was responsible for building the sacred Temple of Jerusalem.

WHY IS THE DOME OF THE ROCK CELEBRATED BY TWO RELIGIONS?

The Dome of the Rock, which stands in Jerusalem, Israel, is worshipped by both the Jews and also the Muslims as a holy shrine.

Firstly, the Jews believe that the Dome of the Rock is built over the rock on which Abraham, on God's orders, prepared to sacrifice his son to Isaac.

Secondly, the Muslims believe that Muhammad rose to heaven from the very same rock.

• FACT FILE •

In this image, Moses, the leader of the Hebrew people, receives the two tablets from God. The stone tablets bear the Ten Commandments, as described in the Old Testament. They became the basis for Jewish law.

WHY DO ISLAMIC BELIEVERS FOLLOW THE KORAN?

The Holy Koran

The Koran is the holy book of the Islamic religion. It contains the words of Allah as revealed to Mohammed by the archangel Jibril (Gabriel) in a series of visions.

The Koran is a collection of verses describing the ways in which Muslims should conduct their lives. It specifies daily prayers, and emphasizes the need for brotherly love and charity between Muslims. Although Muslims do not worship Mohammed, they show him the greatest respect. They believe that the Koran is the word of Allah and was not composed by Mohammed.

?

DID YOU KNOW THAT THE KORAN SHOULD BE KEPT ON THE HIGHEST BOOKSHELF IN THE HOUSE, IN ORDER TO REPRESENT THE FACT THAT IT IS RATED MORE HIGHLY THAN ALL OTHER BOOKS.

WHY DO THE ABORIGINES BELIEVE IN 'DREAMTIME'?

Dreamtime relates to the aborigines of Australia, and their stories of Creation, when ancestral spirits came to Earth and taught people how to live and how to respect the animals and plants that had been created.

The Aborigines retold these stories for generations, capturing them in religious paintings on rocks and in caves across the land. There are also Dreamtime tracks in many places in Australia – paths taken by the spirits.

Today, some Aborigines live in cities, but other communities still maintain a traditional, rural life, living and hunting in 'the bush'. Aborigines only take from the land the animals and plants they need for food.

Before they can become men, young Aboriginal boys make a journey, all alone, into the wilderness to prove they can survive. Their journey is known as a 'walkabout'.

DID YOU KNOW THAT ABORIGINES USED RITUAL BOOMERANGS DECORATED WITH SECRET SYMBOLS IN MAGICAL DANCES?

• FACT FILE •

The giant, red rock Uluru is a sacred site for Australian Aborigines, dating back to the dawn of the world they call Dreamtime. The religious artworks in its caves are thousands of years old, but the paint is continually renewed.

WHERE DOES THE NAME 'DRUID' COME FROM?

The word 'druid' is derived from 'oak'. *Dru-wid* combines the word roots 'oak' and 'knowledge'. It was Pliny the Elder in his *Naturalis Historia* (XVI 95), who associated the Druids with mistletoe and oak groves:

'The Druids . . . hold nothing more sacred than the mistletoe and the tree on which it grows, provided it is an oak. They choose the oak to form groves, and they do not perform any religious rites without its foliage . . .'

Celtic priests, also known as druids, have often been identified as wizards. They performed mysterious rites in sacred groves of trees. The Moon, the oak and mistletoe were all magical to the Druids, and so too were many animals. However, in pre-Christian Celtic society they formed an intellectual class comprising philosophers, judges, educators, historians, doctors, seers, astronomers and astrologers. The earliest surviving classical references to Druids date from the 2nd century BCE.

• FACT FILE •

Around the campfire at night, Celtic poets, storytellers and musicians would pass on tales of the gods and of events in the history of their people.

WHERE DOES THE WORD 'FEUDAL' COME FROM?

Feudalism is the general term used to describe the political and military system of western Europe during the Middle Ages. The word feudal comes from a Latin term for fief. The fief was the estate or land granted by a lord in return for a subject's loyalty and service. Some fiefs were large enough to support one knight; others were great provinces of a kingdom, such as the province of Normandy in France. The Church, which owned large fiefs, was also part of the feudal system. Feudalism began to appear in the 8th century. By the 12th century, it had spread from France into England, Spain and other parts of the Christian world.

• FACT FILE •

A highly ornate gold drinking goblet. Only a very wealthy person could afford such costly items as this. Poorer people drank out of leather tankards or earthenware cups.

WHO LIVED IN A MONASTERY?

After the fall of the Roman Empire, the Christian Church provided the only stable government in Europe. Christian communities took on the work of teaching the faith, education and healing. In this work, monasteries came to play an important part.

Monasteries were the places where the monks lived. Monks wore simple robes, shaved their heads, and shared all their daily tasks. Each monastery was led by an abbot, and the largest ones became the central point, not only of religious life, but also of local power. Monks went to as many as eight church services every day. Monks spent part of their time teaching young boys, who would, in time, become monks themselves. A monk's day was regulated by hours of work, rest and worship.

During the Middle Ages, monasteries frequently housed people as they travelled from one place to another.

? DID YOU KNOW THAT DURING THE MIDDLE AGES, KINGS BELIEVED THAT THEIR RIGHT TO RULE THEIR LAND CAME FROM GOD?

• FACT FILE •

The monastery at Mont Saint-Michel in France was built by Benedictine monks in 966 CE. It stands on a tiny island in Normandy, linked by a causeway to the mainland.

WHAT WERE THE CRUSADES?

Crusades were the military expeditions organized mainly to recapture Palestine during the Middle Ages. Palestine, also called the Holy Land, was important to Christians because it was the region where Jesus Christ had lived. Palestine lay along the eastern coast of the Mediterranean Sea and Muslims had taken control of it from the Christians. The crusaders, who came from western Europe, organized eight major expeditions between 1096 and 1270. This was a period when western Europe was expanding its economy and increasing its military forces. Kings, nobles and thousands of knights, peasants and townspeople took part in the Crusades. They had two main goals: first to gain permanent control of the Holy Land and second to protect the Byzantine Empire.

The last major crusade was called the Children's Crusade in which some claim that 50,000 children set off from France and Germany for the Holy Land. Whether all of them were in fact children is disputed by modern scholars.

WHO WERE
THE TEUTONIC KNIGHTS?

The Teutonic Knights is the name of an organization of German crusaders founded in 1190. The Teutonic Knights modelled their organization on two earlier crusading orders, the Knights Templars and the Knights Hospitallers. The crusades were part of a Christian movement to recapture the Holy Land from the Muslims, in which kings, nobles and thousands of knights, peasants and townspeople took part. In the 13th century, the Teutonic Knights shifted their activities to Central Europe, where they tried to convert and control the people of what became Prussia, Lithuania, Latvia and Estonia. Their power and influence spread throughout Central and Eastern Europe.

In the 14th century, the Teutonic Knights lost much of their power, and were finally overthrown by the Poles and Lithuanians.

DID YOU KNOW THAT THE CRUSADES WERE ORIGINALLY CALLED ARMED PILGRIMAGES? THE WORD 'CRUSADE' CAME LATER, FROM THE LATIN WORD *CRUX*, MEANING CROSS.

• FACT FILE •

At the end of the crusades many of the knights stayed on to guard the conquered land. They were known to build fine castles.

WHAT WAS THE MAGNA CARTA?

The youngest son of Henry II, John, inherited from his brother Richard the throne of England, as well as the Plantagenet dominions of France, which he had lost to the French by 1204. John's failure to recapture these territories, his dispute with Rome over the Pope's choice of a new Archbishop of Canterbury, and a high level of taxation had the English nobility up in arms against him.

In 1215 they forced the king to agree to the Magna Carta, guaranteeing their rights in relation to those of the Crown. It was intended to protect the rights of nobles, and made sure that no-one was imprisoned without a fair trial. Copies of this document, which tried to put an end to the king's abuse of his power, were distributed across the whole of England. This led to civil war, which ended with John's death in 1216.

Despite all these disasters, it is now known that John was a much better king than history has actually portrayed him to have been.

John

• FACT FILE •

This image shows the coronation of Charles V. He became king of Spain in 1516 (he was the grandson of King Ferdinand and Queen Isabella of Spain). Three years later he became Holy Roman Emperor.

WHY DID KING HENRY VIII DEFY THE POPE?

HENRY VIII MARRIED SIX TIMES IN TOTAL! HE DIVORCED TWO WIVES AND BEHEADED TWO. ONE OF HIS WIVES DIED IN CHILDBIRTH, WHILE THE LAST SURVIVED HIM.

• FACT FILE •

Excommunicated by the Pope, Henry gave himself unrestricted power and set about consolidating the spiritual independence of England from Rome. In 1536, Henry VIII ordered that monasteries such as Tintern Abbey be 'dissolved', or closed down and ransacked.

As Martin Luther's ideas of the Reformation spread, reformers, who became known as Protestants, emerged throughout Europe. A theological debate followed that eventually erupted into religious warfare that was to last for well over a century.

In England, Henry VIII initially defended the Catholic Church. However, the lengths to which Henry VIII went to get a male heir shocked Europe. In 1509, he married Catherine of Aragon, but when all her sons died in infancy, Henry wanted the marriage declared invalid.

The Pope refused this request. As a consequence Henry cut all ties between England and the Catholic Church in Rome and declared himself Supreme Head of the Church of England.

WHO WERE THE PILGRIM FATHERS?

The Pilgrim Fathers were the early English settlers of New England in the United States. Originally they were called the Old Comers, then the Forefathers, and were not known as the Pilgrim Fathers until the 19th century. The first group of pilgrims to set sail from England in 1620 left on a ship called the *Mayflower*; they landed in December at what is now Plymouth, Massachusetts on the US east coast. It was here that they established Plymouth Colony along Cape Cod Bay. Only half of their party survived the first winter. In the following summer a feast was held between the settlers and the local Native Americans in thanks for their survival; it was the first Thanksgiving celebration.

Many of the Pilgrim Fathers were Puritans. The Puritans were a religious group who wanted the Church of England to distance itself more fully from Catholicism.

• FACT FILE •

In the colonies, girls would embroider samplers – squares of cloth decorated with words and patterns of needlework. They usually added their name and age, as well as the date.

WHEN WAS THE SLAVE TRADE ABOLISHED IN AFRICA?

During the 1700s the slave trade brought misery to thousands of Africans, who were transported across the Atlantic Ocean and forced to work as slaves on plantations in the Americas. This trade also brought huge wealth to those who ran it – the shipbuilders, ship owners, merchants and traders.

Many people began to condemn the slave trade and to call for it to be abolished. The slave trade came to an end in the British Empire in 1807 and was finally abolished within the empire in 1833.

In 1788 an association was formed in London to encourage British exploration and trade in Africa. Many British explorers set out to explore Africa along its rivers. Probably the most famous of all the expeditions was led by David Livingstone, who set out to look for the source of the River Nile. After being out of contact for almost three years, he was eventually found by the American journalist Henry Stanley.

David Livingstone

A typical colonist's hat

Slavery did not come to an end in the United States until after the American Civil War in 1865, and continued in Brazil until 1889.

• FACT FILE •

The anti-slavery movement was strongest in Britain and the USA. Many abolitionist speakers joined the struggle to gain equal rights for black people.

WHO WERE THE SUFFRAGETTES?

Suffragettes were women who fought for the right to vote at the turn of the 20th century – a time when only men could do so. In wartime, women were brought in to fill the jobs of men who had gone to fight. The poster shown here emphasized the important role women had to play.

In 1893, New Zealand became the first country in the world to allow women to vote in national elections. Australia followed suit in 1903 and Finland in 1906. In other parts of the world, however, women were engaged in a bitter and often violent battle for the right to vote.

In Britain, Emmeline Pankhurst founded the Women's Social and Political Union (WSPU) in 1903. The WSPU believed in actions rather than words, and many of its members, known as suffragettes, were arrested and imprisoned.

For a healthy, happy job

Join the **WOMEN'S LAND ARMY**

for details
APPLY TO NEAREST W.L.A. COUNTY OFFICE OR TO W.L.A HEADQUARTERS 6 CHESHAM STREET LONDON S.W.1

• FACT FILE •

The cover of *Suffragette* magazine laments the loss of Emily Davison. Only in 1928 was suffrage extended to all women over the age of 21 in Britain.

The **Suffragette**

IN HONOUR AND IN LOVING, REVERENT MEMORY OF
EMILY WILDING DAVISON.

One suffragette, Emily Davison, was killed when she threw herself beneath the king's horse at a race.

126 ⇔ TELL ME ABOUT HISTORY

WHO FOUNDED FASCISM?

Benito Mussolini (1883–1945) founded fascism and ruled Italy for almost 21 years, most of that time as a dictator. Mussolini had founded the *Fasci di Combattimento* in 1919. This movement appealed to war veterans with a plan that supported government ownership of national resources and that put the interests of Italy above all others.

In 1921, Mussolini transformed the Fasci into the National Fascist Party, adopting a more conservative scheme to gain the support of property-owning Italians. Mussolini dreamed of building Italy into a great empire, but instead he led his nation to defeat in World War II.

MUSSOLINI MET WITH A BITTER END. DEFEATED BY THE ALLIES TOWARDS THE END OF WORLD WAR II, HE WAS KILLED BY HIS OWN PEOPLE AS HE ATTEMPTED TO FLEE THE COUNTRY.

FACT FILE

Sir Oswald Mosley formed the British Union of Fascists in the 1930s. He and his black-shirted followers were involved in riots, especially in London's East End. In World War II, Mosley was imprisoned for his pro-German views. Later, he tried to revive fascism in the United Kingdom.

WHAT WAS
THE HOLOCAUST?

The main entrance to Auschwitz-Birkenau concentration camp

In the early 1930s, the Nazi party rose to power in Germany, led by Adolf Hitler. He set up a secret police force, banned opposing political parties and started to persecute minority groups in the German population, such as gypsies and Jews.

During World War II, concentration camps such as Belsen and Auschwitz were set up by the Nazis. Millions of Jews were imprisoned and murdered in these camps because Hitler believed they were responsible for the downfall of Germany. Some six million Jews died in these camps in World War II, an event known as the Holocaust.

WHAT IS COMMUNISM?

Communism is a system of political and economic organization in which property is owned by the state and all citizens share the common wealth, more or less according to their needs. After years of civil war, much of China was in ruins. Mao Zedong set about reforming the country according to communist ideals. Land was seized from landowners and divided up among the peasants. In Mao's 'Five-Year Plan' (1953–1957) new roads and railways were built, industry boosted, and health and education improved. Mao printed his ideals about his communist state in what became known as Mao's 'Little Red Book', which was read by millions of Chinese.

Well-known Communist leaders past and present include Vladimir Lenin, Josef Stalin, Fidel Castro, Pol Pot and Nicolae Ceausescu.

• FACT FILE •

Chairman Mao and his supporters accused many people of failing to follow communist ideals. Students and young people formed groups of 'Red Guards' in support of Mao.

WHEN WAS
THE COLD WAR?

• FACT FILE •

Early in 1945 the Allied leaders met in Yalta in the Crimea to decide on the shape of the post-war world. Churchill, Roosevelt and Stalin decided on how Germany was to be split up once the war was won.

After World War II, the United States and the USSR emerged as the two main powers in the world – known as 'superpowers'. Although they had fought together to defeat Nazi Germany, differences between the two superpowers soon led to the start of the 'Cold War'.

The Cold War started in August 1945, and it was a political war between the USSR and its communist allies, and the USA and other non-communist countries. A lot of tension grew between East and West and, with it, the growing threat of nuclear war, although it never actually happened. Instead, the two sides sponsored wars and political unrest in other countries, destabilizing governments of which they disapproved. The closest the world came to nuclear war was in 1962 when the Soviet Union moved missiles into Cuba, directly threatening the United States. The missiles were eventually removed, but only when the Americans threatened retaliation.

? DID YOU KNOW THAT GEORGE ORWELL FIRST USED THE TERM 'COLD WAR' IN AN ESSAY ABOUT THE USE OF THE ATOM BOMB IN 1945?

WHO FOUNDED THE ZIONIST MOVEMENT?

Theodore Herzl died more than 40 years before the creation of the state of Israel.

The Zionist movement was founded by Theodore Herzl in the late 19th century and promoted the establishment of an independent Jewish state in Israel. At the time, Jewish people lived all over the world, particularly in European countries, the United States and Russia, and yet some called for Jews to return to the area around Jerusalem, which they considered their spiritual homeland.

In 1917, the British government issued the Balfour Declaration, offering support for a Jewish homeland in Palestine. Jewish immigration increased rapidly in the 1930s as thousands of Jews fled Nazi persecution. On 14 May 1948, Israel was established as the Jewish homeland and over 40 per cent of the world's Jews now live there.

• FACT FILE •

Israel has borders with Lebanon and Syria, Jordon and Egypt. In 1967 Israel occupied the territories of the Gaza Strip and the West Bank, home to over one million Palestinian Arabs, and the Sinai Peninsula.

WHAT WAS APARTHEID?

The Apartheid Museum, Johannesburg

From 1948 until 1991, the South African government segregated people of different racial origin using a strict system called apartheid, from the Afrikaans word for separateness. Everyone was classified as white, mixed race, black or Asian, and people from the four groups were kept strictly separate: they could not live in the same areas; shop in the same shops; go to the same doctor; attend the same school or even get on the same bus.

Thousands of people were imprisoned for protesting against the system. After years of international pressure, including bars on South African goods being sold abroad and sportsmen and women suffering bans from all international competition, the government finally repealed the last of the apartheid laws in 1991.

• FACT FILE •

In 1962 the United Nations General Assembly urged its members to boycott South Africa to force it to abolish apartheid, which it finally began to do in 1990.

WHY IS
NELSON MANDELA FAMOUS?

Nelson Mandela was an internationally respected figure. In 1942, he joined the African National Congress (ANC), a political party that led the struggle against the injustices of white-minority rule in South Africa. He was imprisoned for conspiracy to overthrow the South African government in 1962 and remained there until 1990.

Over the years, Mandela became a symbol of the struggle against racism. He became President of the ANC in 1991 and negotiated with the government to dismantle apartheid. In 1994, he was elected the first black President of South Africa. He retired in 1999 and used his influence to fight against injustice, racism, poverty and AIDs.

Nelson Mandela died in 2013. He was 95 years old.

• FACT FILE •

The United Nations sends its troops to trouble spots all over the world in order to try to prevent further hostilities. They also restore peace in countries that are suffering from civil war.

WHO INTRODUCED PERESTROIKA AND GLASNOST?

Mikhail Sergeyevich Gorbachev was the leader of the Soviet Union from 1985 to 1991. As Soviet leader, Gorbachev gained worldwide fame for his efforts to make changes in his country and its relations with other nations. In 1990, Gorbachev received the Nobel Peace Prize for his contributions to world peace.

Gorbachev made many proposals to change the Soviet political system to make it, and other parts of the Soviet social system, more open and democratic. He called for a reduction in the power of the Communist Party – which controlled the country – and increased power for elected bodies. His programme of economic and political reform was called *perestroika* (restructuring). His call for more openness was known as *glasnost*.

?

DID YOU KNOW THAT THE SOVIET UNION COLLAPSED IN 1991? AMONG THE 15 COUNTRIES THAT GAINED THEIR INDEPENDENCE ARE ARMENIA, LATVIA, ESTONIA, LITHUANIA AND UKRAINE.

• FACT FILE •

The US president, Ronald Reagan, was a keen supporter of Gorbachev's programme of reforms in the USSR. In 1987 the two leaders signed an agreement to dismantle many kinds of nuclear weapon.

WHEN WAS THE BERLIN WALL DEMOLISHED?

A Trabant appears to burst through the Berlin Wall in a section that has been preserved as an art installation in former East Berlin.

In August 1961, the German Democratic Republic began under the leadership of Erich Honecker to block off East Berlin and the GDR from West Berlin by means of barbed wire and antitank obstacles. Streets were torn up and barricades of paving stones were erected. Tanks gathered at crucial places. The subway and local railway services between East and West Berlin were interrupted. Inhabitants of East Berlin and the GDR were no longer allowed to enter the West.

In the following days, construction brigades began replacing the provisional barriers with a solid wall. This wall stood in place for nearly 30 years. In November 1989, after weeks of discussion about new travel laws, the Berlin Wall was demolished.

• FACT FILE •

With the end of communist rule in the USSR, many of the symbols of communism, for example statues of former leaders such as Lenin and Stalin, were dismantled.

HEROES
AND VILLAINS

CONTENTS

WHY IS
CONFUCIUS REMEMBERED?

Confucius was an ancient Chinese philosopher who taught the need for moral responsibility and virtue. His teachings did not make much impact during his lifetime, but they later became the central part of Chinese moral and religious thinking.

Confucius probably lived from 551 to 479 BCE, in the time of the Zhou dynasty. The Zhou was the longest-lasting group of Chinese rulers, who governed the country from 1122 to 256 BCE. Confucianism was probably the most important feature in Chinese life until the appearance of communism in the 20th century. Confucianism resembles a religion, but instead of worshipping gods it guides on morality and good government.

Although Confucius lived thousands of years ago, his influence in everyday life is still strong in China today.

WHO WAS
ALEXANDER THE GREAT?

DID YOU KNOW THAT ALEXANDER THE GREAT ALSO HAD A FAVOURITE DOG? IT WAS CALLED PERITAS AND ACCOMPANIED ALEXANDER IN ALL OF HIS BATTLES.

Alexander the Great (356–323 BCE) was king of the Macedonians and is remembered as one of the greatest generals in history. He conquered the Persian Empire, which stretched from the Mediterranean Sea to India and formed much of what was then considered the civilized world.

Alexander's conquests advanced the spread of Greek ideas and customs in western Asia and Egypt. According to one story, as a young boy Alexander tamed the great horse Bucephalus, which was said to be too high-spirited and wild to control. This steed later carried Alexander into battle at Issus in 333 BCE. Alexander built a city and named it Bucephala after his horse.

WHO WAS ARCHIMEDES?

Archimedes of Syracuse (287–212 BCE) was a Greek mathematician. He was born and worked in the city of Syracuse in Sicily, although he studied at Alexandria, Egypt. While wondering about how to test if a crown was made of pure gold, Archimedes discovered the principle of buoyancy – if an object is placed in a fluid, it will displace its own volume of that fluid. This is now known as Archimedes' principle.

It was Archimedes who had the original 'Eureka' moment. Getting into his bath he noticed that the water rose up the sides – his body was displacing its own volume of water. He raced into the street, without any clothes, shouting, 'Eureka' (I've found it).

?

DID YOU KNOW THAT ARCHIMEDES WAS AN INVENTOR? HE DEVISED MACHINES THAT COULD HELP HIS COUNTRYMEN IN TIMES OF WAR. ONE USED A SYSTEM OF MIRRORS TO CONCENTRATE SUNLIGHT ON ENEMY SHIPS UNTIL THEY BURST INTO FLAMES!

• FACT FILE •

A means of raising water for irrigation, the Archimedes screw comprises a cylinder with a large screw inside. The bottom of the screw is dipped in water and as the screw is turned, water is pushed up the cylinder.

WHO WAS ASOKA?

The Mauryan Empire reached from the Hindu Kush mountains in Afghanistan to Bangladesh, and from Assam in the east, to Kerala and Andhra Pradesh in south.

The Mauryan Empire was the first empire to provide a single government for almost all of India. Mauryan emperors ruled from about 324 to 185 BCE. Their empire was built around Magadha, a rich kingdom in the Ganges Valley. This empire was ruled from about 324 to around 298 BCE by Chandragupta Maurya. Asoka was his grandson, and the greatest emperor of ancient India. He took government very seriously, reforming taxes, encouraging trade and farming, and building walled cities with pleasant houses and paved streets. His officials travelled the country, building roads and collecting taxes from peasant farmers in the villages.

Asoka was born a Hindu, but he became a Buddhist. He then gave up war, sickened by the slaughter he had seen during his conquest of Orissa in the southeast. Asoka made new laws and had them inscribed on stone pillars set up all across his empire.

WHO WAS PTOLEMY OF ALEXANDRIA?

Ptolemy of Alexandria was an ancient Greek astronomer, who lived from around 87 to 150 CE. He wrote many books containing Greek ideas and observations collected over the past 500 years, including *Almagest* ('The Greatest'/'The Mathematical Collection').

Ptolemy described more than 1,000 stars in his books, including 48 different constellations. He also made early calculations of the size and distance of the sun and the Moon. Ptolemy devised a geocentric system with Earth at the centre of the Sun, Moon, planets and stars, although he did not distinguish the differences between them. His order for closest to furthest from Earth read: the Moon, Mercury, Venus, the Sun, Mars, Jupiter and Saturn.

?

DID YOU KNOW THAT PTOLEMY ALSO STUDIED GEOGRAPHY? HE WAS AMONG THE FIRST TO USE A GRID TO SPAN THE GLOBE, USING LINES OF LATITUDE AND LONGITUDE.

• FACT FILE •

English mathematician Sir Issac Newton developed the reflecting telescope in 1669.

WHY IS
BOADICEA REMEMBERED?

Boadicea (Boudicca) was the queen of the Iceni, a tribe of Celts living in eastern England. Her husband was a governor, who worked with the Romans. After his death, the Romans tried to take control. Boadicea led a rebellion, which sacked the towns of Colchester and London, until the Roman armies marched against her. The Romans defeated the Iceni and their Celtic allies.

Boadicea is renowned for fighting from a chariot, and the Romans had to develop special tactics to combat these fast-moving warriors.

BOADICEA ENDED HER OWN LIFE BY TAKING POISON TO AVOID BEING CAPTURED!

• FACT FILE •

Celtic poetry -
'STORM AT SEA'
Tempest on the plain of Lir
Bursts its barriers far and near
And upon the rising tide
Wind and noisy winter ride
Winter throws a shining spear.

WHY WAS ATTILA THE HUN SO FEARED?

Attila was the ruler of the Hun kingdom, in what is now called Hungary. The Huns began to expand beyond this area, conquering surrounding countries until they controlled a region from the Rhine to the Caspian Sea, extending all the way to the Baltic.

The Huns were among the fiercest of the barbarian tribes who destroyed the power of the Roman Empire. Attila, who is still renowned for his cruelty and the ferocity of his troops, led the Huns from their homeland and almost conquered Europe. He forced the Eastern Roman Empire to pay him a fee in exchange for not attacking them. He also demanded to marry the sister of the emperor of the Western Empire, with half the empire as a dowry – a request that was refused and caused bloodshed.

NO ONE REALLY KNOWS HOW ATTILA THE HUN DIED, BUT LEGEND HAS IT THAT HE DIED WHILE HE WAS SLEEPING ON HIS WEDDING NIGHT – FROM A NOSEBLEED!

FACT FILE

Every year, in the village of Bugac, Hungary, a three-day festival is held in celebration of the traditional horse riding, archery and folklore of the Huns.

WHO WAS
ALFRED THE GREAT?

Alfred the Great (849–899) was king of the West Saxons in southwestern England. He saved his kingdom, Wessex, from the Danish Vikings and laid the basis for the unification of England under the West Saxon monarchy. He also led a revival of learning and literature. He was an outstanding leader in both war and peace.

Alfred became king in 871, after the death of his brother Ethelred. He built forts and fortified towns at strategic points. He stationed his fleet along the coast as protection against further invasions from the Danes. He also issued a code of laws to restore peaceful government and encouraged the translation of famous Christian books from Latin into English.

DID YOU KNOW THAT ALFRED IS THE ONLY ENGLISH KING TO BE KNOWN AS 'THE GREAT'?

• FACT FILE •

The Alfred jewel was found near Athelney in Somerset in 1693. It may be part of a bookmark. On it are the words 'Alfred had me made' in Latin.

WHO WAS
WILLIAM THE CONQUEROR?

William I (c. 1027–1087), known as the Conqueror, was the first Norman king of England. He took power in 1066, following his victory over the Anglo-Saxons. As king, he maintained tight control over the country's central government.

William was born at Falaise, in Normandy in northwestern France. He was the son of Robert I, Duke of Normandy, and inherited Normandy in 1035, at about the age of eight.

During his youth there were many uprisings. In 1047, William put down a great rebellion at the battle of Val-es-dunes, near Caen, with the aid of his lord, King Henry I of France. From this time on William ruled Normandy with an iron hand. He took lands from those who resisted him and kept some of these lands for himself and gave the rest to his followers in return for military service.

William the Conqueror was cousin to Edward the Confessor, one of the last Anglo-Saxon kings of England. He used this relationship as the basis for claiming the throne.

FACT FILE

A crucial battle was fought on 14 October 1066, at Senlac Hill, north of Hastings. The English, who fought on foot, resisted bravely as Norman cavalry charged their wall of shields, and archers fired showers of arrows at them. The battle is re-enacted annually on the original site.

WHEN WAS THE ERA OF GENGHIS KHAN?

In the year 1167, a child called Temujin was born on the desolate plains of Mongolia. When the boy was nine, his father was murdered and his family was left poor and friendless. From this grim beginning Temujin grew up to become one of the world's greatest conquerors. He was later hailed by the Mongols as Genghis Khan – the 'Universal Ruler'.

In 1206, Genghis Khan became leader of all the Mongol people, and began to build his astonishing empire. He was a ruthless warrior, destroying entire cities and their populations during his conquests. Yet he succeeded in keeping the peace. Genghis Khan died of a fever in 1227, but the Mongols continued to build up the empire.

GENGHIS KHAN INSTRUCTED THAT HE SHOULD BE BURIED IN AN UNMARKED GRAVE, THE LOCATION OF WHICH WAS NEVER TO BE KNOWN. ANYONE WHO KNEW OF ITS LOCATION IS SAID TO HAVE BEEN KILLED!

• FACT FILE •

The Mongols lived on the flat, grassy steppes of Asia, wandering with their herds of sheep, goats and cattle. They lived in tentlike felt homes, called yurts.

WHY WAS TIMUR LANG NOTORIOUS?

Timur Lang (or Timur the Lame), who claimed to be a descendant of Genghis Khan was a ruthless conqueror. When the Ottomans tried to expand their empire eastwards there was a nasty shock in store for them. Timur had already conquered Persia and ravaged much of central Asia, including Russia and India, before the Ottomans attacked.

Timur fell on the Turks like a hurricane, ransacking their chief city in Anatolia, wiping out their army and capturing their leader. Then he began to loot their empire and break it up. That might have been the end of the Ottoman story, but in 1405 Timur died and the last of the Mongol kingdoms fell apart.

A statue or Timur Lang in Samarkand, Uzbekistan

FACT FILE

When Timur seized the city of Isfahan in 1387, he ordered his men to execute all 7,000 citizens and pile their heads in huge mounds outside the city walls.

SOME REPORTS SAY THAT TIMUR LANG WAS RESPONSIBLE FOR THE DEATHS OF 17 MILLION PEOPLE!

WHO INVENTED
THE PRINTING PRESS?

Throughout history, books have been rare and precious things, kept in libraries of monasteries or wealthy houses. Each one had to be copied out by hand with pen and ink, so very few people had the chance to learn to read.

The Chinese developed a simple system of printing in the 11th century, but it was only in about 1450 that a German named Johannes Gutenberg built the first true printing press.

Using movable metal type, Gutenberg was able to make exact copies of books very cheaply. The first books he printed were the Bible and other religious works. Soon other printers started, and by 1500 they were producing many different sorts of literature, including poems and stories. For the first time, books were available to everyone.

FACT FILE

In about 500 CE monks would spend endless hours on illuminated handwritten books. The work was slow and painstaking, but worthwhile because it was another way for them to show dedication to God.

WHO WAS THE MAID OF ORLEANS?

The Maid of Orleans was Joan of Arc (1412–1431), a French nationalist heroine who became a saint of the Roman Catholic Church. She was a simple peasant girl who rescued France from defeat in one of the darkest periods of the Hundred Years' War with England. Her first great triumph was to lead a French army against the English who had laid siege to the city of Orléans.

Jeanne d'Arc, as she is known in France, was born at Domrémy, near Nancy. She was a strong and healthy child. Like most peasants at that time, she never learned to read or write. She grew up as a devout Catholic under the strong influence of her deeply religious mother. The girl called herself Jeanne la Pucelle (Joan the Maid). By the age of 13, Joan was having religious visions that persuaded her that God had chosen her to help King Charles VII of France drive the English from France. The English saw Joan as an agent of the devil, and she was burned at the stake before a large crowd in Rouen on 30 May, 1431.

JOAN OF ARC'S FORCES BROKE THE SIEGE OF ORLÉANS IN ONLY TEN DAYS!

FACT FILE

Joan set out with her army in April 1429 to rescue Orléans from the English. At first, the French commanders hesitated to obey her. However, they soon realized that all went well when they followed her orders.

WHY WERE LEONARDO DA VINCI'S IDEAS AHEAD OF HIS TIME?

Da Vinci's sketch for a helicopter

Da Vinci was apprenticed to a sculptor, and worked as a painter for the rulers of Florence, Milan and France. He produced several famous paintings, including the Mona Lisa.

During the Renaissance period scientists and inventors were making important discoveries. They were asking questions that would change our view of the Earth – and the heavens – forever. Of course not all the inventions actually worked. The great artist and engineer Leonardo da Vinci was determined to find a way of making people fly like birds.

Throughout his life Leonardo da Vinci drew many designs for flying machines. Among these was a kind of parachute and a helicopter with spinning blades. His grandest idea was for an aircraft with flapping wings, which he dreamed up in about 1503.

He organized a test flight but according to legend the machine crashed. The first successful aircraft did not actually fly for another 400 years, so he was certainly well ahead of his time.

• FACT FILE •

Leonardo da Vinci filled sketchbook after sketchbook with illustrations of all kinds. Among his drawings were studies of human anatomy to help him render the human form with great accuracy in his paintings.

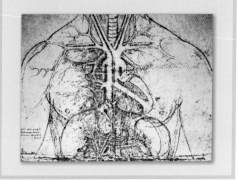

WHY IS
COPERNICUS REMEMBERED?

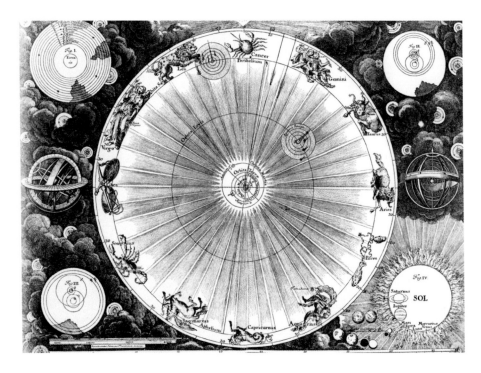

Nicolaus Copernicus was a Polish astronomer. Pictured above is his view of the Universe. He proposed that it was the sun – not the Earth – that was at the centre of the Universe. The Earth and the other planets simply revolved around it.

His idea was proved correct in the 1620s when the Italian Galileo Galilei used an early telescope to observe the planet Jupiter. He could clearly see that there were other moons in orbit round Jupiter. Here were bodies that were not moving round the Earth. This meant one thing: that the Earth was not the centre of the Universe.

The name given to the model of the Universe in which the planets revolve around the Sun is 'heliocentric'.

 **FACT FILE**

Galileo's telescopes were more powerful than any that had been used before. He was the first person to study the night sky through a telescope.

WHO BECAME 'THE MAGNIFICENT' OTTOMAN SULTAN?

In 1520, the greatest of the Ottoman rulers came to the throne. His name was Suleiman, and he was soon to become known as 'The Magnificent' because of the splendour of his court and the might of his armies. His capital Constantinople, renamed Istanbul, was the biggest city in the world. Suleiman set out to expand his empire even further. He captured cities as far afield as Belgrade, Baghdad and Algiers, as well as Aden and the island of Rhodes. In 1526 he smashed the forces of the Hungarian king at the battle of Mohacz. Meanwhile his navy ruled the Mediterranean.

Suleiman was also known as al-Qanuni, 'the law-giver'. He had complete control over the daily lives of his subjects, and chose slaves from his own bodyguard to govern provinces of the empire. He reformed the legal system, so that land rents and taxes were collected properly.

Even after his death in 1566, the Ottoman Empire continued to grow.

• FACT FILE •

Suleiman's empire brought him great wealth, which he used to employ the best artists and architects. Among them was Mirman Sinan, who designed at least 165 mosques and palaces, including the Suleymaniye Mosque in Istanbul (pictured).

Suleiman was not just a fine leader and warrior, he was also a poet and a scholar.

WHO WAS
FRANCISCO PIZARRO?

In the mid -1520s, the Spanish adventurer Francisco Pizarro began to explore the west coast of South America. He had heard tales of the Inca Empire and its gold and silver treasure. In about 1527, Pizarro and a few of his followers landed near the Inca city of Tumbes on Peru's north coast; they became the first white men to set foot in Peru.

Pizarro saw enough treasure at Tumbes to convince him that the legends about the Inca were true. He returned in 1532 with about 180 men, who were later joined by other Spanish troops. By the end of 1533, the Spanish had easily conquered most of Peru, including the fabulous city of Cusco, the Inca capital. In 1535, Pizarro founded Lima, which became the centre of the Spanish government in South America.

By 1550 Spain ruled most of Central and South America and the West Indies. Fleets of Spanish galleons carried gold, silver and plundered treasures across the Atlantic to Europe.

WHO WAS FERDINAND MAGELLAN?

Ptolemy's *Geography*

Ferdinand Magellan was a Portuguese sea captain who commanded the first expedition that sailed around the world. His voyage provided the first positive proof that the Earth is round. Many scholars consider his voyage the greatest navigational feat in history.

People probably made rough maps even before they began to use written language some 5,500 years ago. Over the centuries, maps became more accurate as people explored the world and developed better ways to make maps. It was not until Magellan's voyage in the late 15th century that European scholars agreed that the world was round. An early map of the world appeared in a 1482 edition of Ptolemy's eight-volume *Geography*.

WHO WAS
GALILEO GALILEI?

The son of a musician, Galileo Galilei (1564–1642) went to the University of Pisa to study medicine, but eventually became a professor of mathematics. Galileo is widely considered to be the founder of modern experimental science. He established the principle that scientific theories should be based on data (measurements) obtained from experiments. Galileo was able to devise a mathematical formula to describe the motion of falling objects. The story that he dropped identical weights of iron and feathers from the Leaning Tower of Pisa may not be true, but Galileo did establish that all objects fall at the same speed, no matter what their weight.

Galileo was also interested in astronomy and, though he did not invent the telescope, he did build his own version, in 1609. Galileo was able to observe the craters on our Moon, he discovered Jupiter's four largest moons, and he was the first person to describe the rings of Saturn.

Galileo is a hero of modern science today and has featured on bank notes and stamps.

WHAT WAS
REMBRANDT FAMOUS FOR?

A statue of Rembrandt in Amsterdam

**REMBRANDT WAS A GREAT
COLLECTOR OF ART AND
SPENT SO MUCH MONEY ON
HIS HOBBY THAT HE FELL
INTO SERIOUS DEBT!**

Rembrandt (1606 to 1669) was a Dutch baroque artist, who ranks as one of the greatest painters in the history of Western art. His full name was Rembrandt Harmensz van Rijn. He possessed a profound understanding of human nature that was matched by a brilliant technique – not only in painting but in drawing and etching – and his work made an enormous impact on his contemporaries and influenced the style of many later artists. Rembrandt, born in Leiden on 15 July, 1606, was the son of a miller. Despite the fact that he came from a family of relatively modest means, his parents took great care with his education. Rembrandt began his studies at the Latin School, and at the age of 14 he was enrolled at the Leiden University.

• FACT FILE •

The Renaissance was an art movement that flourished from the 14th to the 17th centuries and is mostly associated with the Italian city of Florence. Its best-known artists include Michelangelo, Leonardo da Vinci, Giotto and Raphael.

WHO WAS VOLTAIRE?

Voltaire was a French philosopher and writer with a keen sense of justice. In the 17th and 18th centuries, a period called the Age of Reason, many people began to regard freedom of speech as a natural right. Such philosophers as John Locke of England and Voltaire of France believed in the importance of the individual. Every person, they declared, had a right to speak freely and to have a voice in the government. Because of these beliefs and for criticizing the government, Voltaire was imprisoned for 11 months in the notorious Bastille prison. The Bastille was a great fortress in Paris that stood as a symbol of royal tyranny. Voltaire wrote more than 50 plays as well as philosophical stories and poems.

VOLTAIRE WAS A KEEN DRINKER OF COFFEE. SOME REPORTS SUGGEST THAT HE DRANK AS MANY AS 50 CUPS OF COFFEE A DAY.

• FACT FILE •

Voltaire was often a guest at Frederick II's court from 1750–1753. Frederick II, pictured here, was the third King of Prussia, and became known as Frederick the Great.

WHO WAS
CARL LINNAEUS?

Carl Linnaeus (1707–1778) was a Swedish botanist and explorer who was the first to create a uniform system for naming plants and animals. Most plants and animals have popular names that vary from place to place. Scientific names are given so that the same name is recognized everywhere. Latin is the language used for scientific names. The scientific names are in two parts. The first is the generic name, which describes a group of related living things, and the second name is the specific name, which applies only to that living thing.

Examples of the scientific names for things include: *Panthera tigris* (tiger); *Elephas maximus* (Asian elephant); *Vanessa atalanta* (red admiral butterfly); and *Muscardinus avellanarius* (common dormouse)

WHO DISCOVERED AUSTRALIA?

In 1768, the British government sent an expedition to find the mysterious southern continent. Its leader was James Cook, and his ship was a small but tough vessel called *Endeavour*. After visiting the island of Tahiti, Cook sailed southwards and then west until he sighted an unknown land.

It turned out to be New Zealand. The *Endeavour* sailed on, searching for the east coast of Australia. By 1770 Cook reached the coast of what he knew to be Australia. He followed it northwards until he found a suitable place to land. He called this Botany Bay.

DID YOU KNOW THAT, OF ALL OF THE EXPLORERS FROM THIS PERIOD, CAPTAIN JAMES COOK EXPLORED AND MAPPED THE MOST TERRITORY?

• FACT FILE •

In 1776, Cook set sail to find a sea passage from the Pacific round the north of America to the Atlantic. Ice blocked his way. He was the first European to reach Hawaii, where he was killed in 1779.

WHO WAS MARY ANNING?

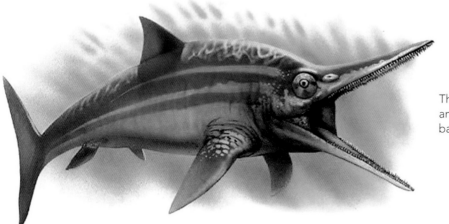

This illustration of an ichthyosaur is based on fossil finds

Englishwoman Mary Anning was a professional fossil collector, working on the shores of Lyme Regis in England in the 1820s. She supplied the greatest scientists of the period with their material and during her career discovered fossils of plesiosaurs, ichthyosaurs and the first pterosaur in Britain. She was one of several palaeontologists working in Britain at the time. The first-ever fossils found in England include fossils of a jawbone and teeth found in Oxfordshire, in around 1815. William Buckland of Oxford University studied the fossils and deduced that they were from a large, meat-eating reptile. In 1822, Buckland's colleague James Parkinson named the creature megalosaurus (big lizard).

The term 'dinosauria' was invented in 1842. English scientist Sir Richard Owen used it to describe the megalosaurus and two other fossil animals, iguanodon and hylaeosaurus, found at the time.

• FACT FILE •

Charles Doolittle Walcott was a vertebrate palaeontologist working in the United States. In 1909, he discovered the Burgess Shale, packed with Cambrian fossils, many of which were of animals that don't seem to fit into any established classification.

WHO WAS
CHARLES DARWIN?

A statue of Charles Darwin at London's Natural History Museum

Darwin was a naturalist and geologist who developed the theory of evolution. In his travels to far-flung places he collected a number of animal and plant specimens, which he turned over to cataloguing experts in Cambridge and London. In South America he had found fossils of extinct armadillos that were similar, but not identical, to the living animals he had seen.

On 24 November 1859, Darwin published his theories in a book called *On The Origin of Species*. It caused a great sensation, but it was some time before it was accepted by the scientific world. The first edition sold out immediately and by 1872 the work had run through six editions. It became generally accepted that evolution took place along the lines that Darwin suggested. His theory on evolution of species solved many puzzles.

DARWIN'S FATHER WAS A DOCTOR AND WANTED HIS SON TO FOLLOW IN HIS FOOTSTEPS, BUT A FEAR OF BLOOD FORCED CHARLES TO DROP OUT OF MEDICAL SCHOOL!

FACT FILE

We can see how evolution has changed living things by examining fossils. Fossils preserve the body parts of living creatures from long ago so that we can see how they have changed over millions of years.

WHO GAVE THE GETTYSBURG ADDRESS?

The Gettysburg Address was given by Abraham Lincoln (1809–1865), 16th president of the United States and one of the great leaders in American history. A humane, far-sighted statesman in his lifetime, he became a legend and a folk hero following his death.

The Gettysburg Address was a short speech that Lincoln delivered during the American Civil War at the site of the Battle of Gettysburg in Pennsylvania.

He delivered the address on 19 November 1863, at ceremonies to dedicate a part of the battlefield as a cemetery for those who had lost their lives in the battle. Lincoln made the address to define the purpose of the war for the people of the northern states and to ensure that the battle would be seen to be a triumph of the Union.

ABRAHAM LINCOLN WAS SHOT WHILE WATCHING A PERFORMANCE AT FORD'S THEATRE IN WASHINGTON! HE LATER DIED FROM HIS WOUNDS.

FACT FILE

Lincoln was against slavery, and his election convinced the leaders of the Southern states that their only option was to leave the Union. South Carolina was the first to leave, followed by Mississippi, Florida, Alabama, Georgia and Louisiana.

WHO WAS
GENERAL CUSTER?

George Armstrong Custer first came to prominence as a cavalry officer during the American Civil War (1861–1865). In 1866 he led the 7th Cavalry against the Native Americans of the Great Plains, and in 1874 he led an expedition that discovered gold in the Black Hills of the Dakota Territory and started a gold rush. The hills were sacred to the Cheyenne and Sioux Indians and relations between these people and the white invaders deteriorated. In 1876, Custer led the 7th Cavalry against an alliance of Cheyenne and Sioux warriors. He went into battle against thousands of warriors in the valley of the Little Bighorn River. He and his main unit of 250 soldiers were all killed in what became known as 'Custer's Last Stand'.

The Battle of Little Bighorn

If you visit the battlefield at Little Bighorn today, you will find memorials to the US soldiers and the Native Americans who lost their lives there.

FACT FILE

Bold pioneers made their way in long trains of covered wagons, drawn by the stories of gold in the hills. However, very few of them actually made their fortunes.

WHY IS FLORENCE NIGHTINGALE REMEMBERED?

Florence Nightingale was an English nurse who single-handedly revolutionized nursing practices, sanitation in hospitals and public health in the 19th century.

When war broke out in the Crimea, Nightingale volunteered for duty, leaving with 38 nurses in her charge. She organized the barracks hospital after the Battle of Inkerman, and by introducing discipline and hygiene to hospitals she managed to reduce the death toll. When she returned to England in 1856, she was rewarded with a fund of £50,000 for training nurses.

DID YOU KNOW THAT FLORENCE NIGHTINGALE USED POLAR DIAGRAMS TO HELP IDENTIFY THE REASONS FOR HOSPITAL DEATHS? THESE WERE A LITTLE LIKE PIE CHARTS.

• FACT FILE •

Florence Nightingale was known as the 'Lady with the Lamp' because of the light she carried at night. She would walk through the hospital corridors, checking on her patients.

WHO WAS
SAMUEL MORSE?

Morse code telegraph station

Samuel Morse was an American famous for inventing the Morse code, in 1838. He first got the idea in 1832 when he was told about experiments with electricity. Morse's idea was to develop a code based on interrupting the flow of electricity so that a message could be heard. Morse code works very simply. Electricity is either switched on or off. When it is on, it travels along a wire. At the other end of the wire the electric current can either make a sound or be printed out. A short electric current, a 'dit', is printed as a dot and a longer 'dah' is printed as a dash. The full Morse code is based on combining dots and dashes to represent the letters of the alphabet.

• FACT FILE •

The telegraph was invented in 1794 by Claude Chappe. France was at war at the time and a quick way to warn of an invasion was needed. Chappe's telegraph used two arms at the top of a tall tower. Ropes and pulleys moved the arms into different positions, each representing a letter. The towers were positioned 10–30km (6–18 miles) apart and the messages were read by people using telescopes.

?

DID YOU KNOW THAT SAMUEL MORSE WAS AN ACCOMPLISHED PORTRAIT PAINTER AS WELL AS BRILLIANT INVENTOR?

WHY DID
GARIBALDI UNIFY ITALY?

?

DID YOU KNOW
THAT THE
DISPARATE
STATES OF THE
GERMAN EMPIRE
WERE UNIFIED IN
1871, MAKING THE
SINGLE COUNTRY
OF GERMANY?

The Treaty of Paris that brought the Crimean War to an end did little to bring stability to Europe. The leader of Sardinia-Piedmont, Count Cavour, used the meetings at Paris to demand unification for Italy. At that time, Italy was made up of many separate states, most controlled by Austria. The movement for independence, known as the Risorgimento, started in the 1820s and 1830s.

In 1858, Sardinia-Piedmont allied itself with France and drove out the Austrians from much of northern Italy. The successful revolt by Guiseppe Garibaldi and his 'red shirts' led eventually to the unification of all of Italy.

Italy was declared a kingdom under King Victor-Emmanuel II in 1861. Rome was captured and made the capital of a unified Italy in 1871.

• FACT FILE •

In Paris, in 1848, people took to the streets to demand a new republic as well as votes for all males. Government soldiers shot and killed some of the rioters.

WHICH EMPEROR MODERNIZED JAPAN?

Japan embarked on a programme of modernization under Emperor Mutsuhito in the 1870s. The 1860s had been a time of uncertainty and political unrest in Japan. Finally, in 1868, the situation became so serious that Emperor Mutsuhito took control from the last shogun. Mutsuhito became known as the Meiji emperor, and this event is called the 'Meiji restoration'. In 1872, a group of Japanese politicians went on a tour of Europe and North America to learn more about industry, education and ways of life in the West. As a result, factories were built in Japan and the country started to change from an agricultural to an industrialized nation. This also included the establishment of a national railway system. During the period of Meiji rule, education was introduced for all Japanese people. The Meiji emperor also gave farmers ownership of their lands and changed Japan's army and navy into modern military forces.

The emperor took the name Meiji ('enlightened rule') as his reign name.

FACT FILE

During the Meiji period, Japan wanted to extend its territories. In 1894–1895 its forces crushed the Chinese navy and gained control of Taiwan. Here you can see a Chinese ship sinking during the Battle of Yalu in 1894.

WHO LED INDIA TO INDEPENDENCE?

Civil rights leader, Mohandas Gandhi led India to independence. During the first half of the 20th century, Gandhi recognized that many Indians wanted independence from British rule, and a chance to build up industry and wealth in India itself.

By the end of World War II it was clear that Britain could no longer ignore the demands of the Indian people. Gandhi tried to talk to the British government, but negotiations were complicated by the demands of Muslims in India. Violence broke out between Hindus and Muslims, and Indians and British leaders eventually agreed to divide India into the two states of Hindu India and Muslim Pakistan. India gained its independence in August 1947. Millions of Hindus and Muslims fled from their homes. As people tried to move to their new homes hundreds of thousands of people were killed.

In 1930 Gandhi led hundreds on a 386-km (240-mile) march across India to the sea, where they made salt from saltwater. This was a protest against the Salt Acts, which made it a crime to possess salt not bought from the government.

• FACT FILE •

In the middle of the Indian flag is an ancient symbol of a wheel. It is known as the Dharma Chakra, which means the 'Wheel of Law'. India gained her independence from Britain on 15 August, 1947.

WHICH PRESIDENT LED THE US OUT OF THE GREAT DEPRESSION?

A disastrous stock market crash in 1929 in the United States left many people penniless overnight. The effects of the Wall Street Crash were felt all over the world. Many countries in Europe were hard hit because they had borrowed money from the United States at the end of World War I. Throughout the 1930s, unemployment soared and trade slumped in a period known as the Great Depression. During the worst years of the depression, many people were forced to rely on charity and government handouts for their most basic needs. In 1932 Franklin D Roosevelt was elected US president. His 'New Deal' aimed to create jobs and to protect people's savings by regulating banks more closely. The US economy went from strength to strength from 1933 to 1937 and was boosted once more when meeting demands servicing World War II.

• FACT FILE •

This is the Stock Exchange in Wall Street at the time of its collapse. You can see brokers spilling out onto the streets of the city of New York.

WHO MADE THE WORLD'S FIRST POWERED FLIGHT?

A full-size model of the Wright brothers' plane stands as a memorial in North Carolina

The world's first powered flight was made by American brothers, Wilbur and Orville Wright. In 1899 Wilbur, while watching birds, realized that an aeroplane must be able to bank to one side or another, to climb or descend, and to steer to the left or right. On 17 December 1903, the brothers travelled to sand dunes outside Kitty Hawk in North Carolina with their plane, *Flyer*. Wilbur ran alongside holding one wing to balance the plane while Orville operated the controls lying face down on the lower wing. The flight lasted just 12 seconds and covered a distance of 36.5m (120ft). Their historic moment was witnessed by just five people.

WHO WERE THE FIRST MEN TO CLIMB EVEREST?

• FACT FILE •

Many animals that live in tropical, temperate and cold regions live in the Himalayas. Tigers, leopards, rhinoceroses, elephants, yaks and several kinds of monkey can all be found living there.

Sir Edmund Percival Hillary, a mountaineer from New Zealand, and Nepalese Sherpa mountaineer, Tenzing Norgay were the first men to reach the summit of Mount Everest, on 29 May 1953. Everest is the tallest mountain on Earth and can be found in the Himalayas – a vast mountain range formed by the crumpling of the Earth's surface as India moves northwards and collides with Asia.

The Himalayas form an arc 2,410km (1,500 miles) long between India, Pakistan and China, with Nepal perched among them. Besides Everest are Kanchenjunga, K2 and Nanga Parbat in the Karakoram range, a northwestern extension of the Himalayas.

AS MANY AS 4,000 PEOPLE HAVE REACHED EVEREST'S SUMMIT SINCE HILLARY AND NORGAY FIRST SCALED THE MOUNTAIN!

WHO WAS JFK?

JFK was the 35th president of the United States. The initials stand for John F. Kennedy (his middle name was Fitzgerald). He was 43 years old when he became president. He and his fashionable wife, Jackie, appealed to a younger generation of Americans, who supported his political views. Kennedy had a difficult time in office, confronting communist Russia over the Cuban Missile Crisis of 1962 and facing harsh criticism for sending troops to fight a war in Vietnam. Highlights of his time as president include his initiation of the Apollo space programme, which went on to land the first men on the Moon, and his tremendous support for the civil rights movement for racial equality.

• FACT FILE •

At 12.30 p.m. on 22 November 1963, John F. Kennedy was assassinated while on a presidential visit to Dallas, Texas. His death left the United States in deep shock. He had been president of the United States for barely 1,000 days. Owing to his achievements while in office and the untimely nature of his death, JFK has become a 20th-century icon.

The book depository in Dallas, from which shots are thought to have been fired.

Kennedy was the fourth US president to be assassinated. Before him, Abraham Lincoln, James A. Garfield and William McKinley all met their deaths while serving in office.

WHO WAS THE FIRST MAN IN SPACE?

The first cosmonaut was the Russian, Yuri Gagarin, who made the first-ever manned spaceflight on 12 April 1961. On the way back down to Earth, Gagarin was ejected from his capsule at a height of 7,000m (23,000ft) and landed by parachute.

The first manned spaceflight lasted less than two hours from launch to landing. Since that time, people have travelled into space in a variety of different spacecraft. While the first manned spacecraft was just big enough to fit one person inside, later spacecraft could fly three people around the world or take them all the way to the Moon and back. Until 2003, Russia and the United States were the only countries with a manned space programme, but in that year China launched its first manned space mission. *Shenzhou-5* carried Yang Liwei into space on 15 October. He returned home after orbiting Earth 14 times.

Первый человек, проникший в космос,—
гражданин Союза Советских Социалистических Республик
Герой Советского Союза летчик-космонавт СССР
Юрий Алексеевич ГАГАРИН.

FACT FILE

Vostok was the first manned spacecraft and the culmination of a space race between the United States and the Soviet Union. The *Vostok* capsule was a small sphere only 2.5m (8ft) across and carried one cosmonaut into space for missions lasting up to five days.